The Miracle
of Grace

The Miracle
of Grace
and Other Messages

D. Martyn Lloyd-Jones

BAKER BOOK HOUSE
Grand Rapids, Michigan 49506

ISBN: 0-8010-5636-5

Printed in the United States of America

Unless otherwise indicated, all Scripture quotations contained herein are from the King James Version (KJV) of the Bible.

Contents

Introduction

Recently, while looking at a volume of the *Christian World Pulpit* from my library, I came across one of D. Martyn Lloyd-Jones' sermons. I was prompted to search through other volumes of the *Christian World Pulpit* and fortunately I found in them other sermons by the eminent Dr. Lloyd-Jones.

I was excited because I had uncovered a treasure I never knew existed but yet I had it in my possession for many years. Certainly it is satisfying to pass on to you these "nuggets of gold." Even the Lloyd-Jones family members were not aware of their existence.

I found three sermons especially inspiring. In "Sin and Its Consequences" Lloyd-Jones says: "The Israelite's statement regarding the manna reveals not only ignorance, but also arrogance. They contemptuously referred to 'this manna.'" In "Living Near to God" Lloyd-Jones states: "The moment we get away from God everything will go wrong. . . . In the presence of God we are lifted up above our circumstances." In "The Miracle of Grace" is this declaration: "The amount of blessing which we would possess depends entirely on ourselves. 'Go borrow the vessels of *all* thy neighbors.' Not just one here and there. God was going to work a miracle, therefore, she must get hold of every single vessel she could.''

May your appreciation of D. Martyn Lloyd-Jones' messages grow. May the messages benefit and enrich your life.

Ernest Eugene Jolley
Birmingham, Alabama
May, 1986

1

The Miracle of Grace

And it came to pass, when the vessels were full, that
she said unto her son, Bring me yet a vessel. And he
said unto her, There is not a vessel more. And the
oil stayed. (2 Kings 4:6)

I want to direct your attention to that well-
known incident of the widow and the cruse of oil, recorded
in the Second Book of Kings (4:1–7), that through it we may
see what constitutes the essence of the Christian religion,
and, therefore, of the Christian life.

It may seem a rather curious thing to deal with such a
subject by means of a text from the Old Testament rather
than from the New. Yet we must agree that the Old
Testament contains essentially the same message as does the
New, the only difference being that the message is much
clearer in the New Testament; there we have the same
message presented to us in a different form and with a
greater fullness than in the Old.

There is, I think, a distinct advantage in going to the Old
Testament to consider the essence of the New Testament

Preached in Westminster Chapel

message; the Old Testament generally presents the truth in the form of a picture. And if we look at the Old Testament with New Testament eyes we actually find the truth there in a form that is particularly clear.

I ought to preface my remarks by stating that I'll not be dealing with justification by faith. I am going to take that for granted. Many of us have been prone to identify the whole of Christianity with just that one doctrine. Many people seem to think that Christianity is a message which announces forgiveness of sin—and we thank God that there is that initial doctrine of forgiveness, for without it we were all undone—but God forbid that we should imagine that that is the whole of Christianity, that we should think of Christianity's great eternal message merely as something that saves us from punishment and suffering; it starts with forgiveness, but it goes on to offer us something which in a sense is infinitely greater, and it is to that second aspect that I am anxious to direct your attention.

Defining Christianity

That great man of God, John Wesley, was fond of saying toward the end of his career, that of all the definitions of Christianity he had encountered, the best was that of a Scotsman who lived in the seventeenth century: "Christianity is the life of God in the soul of man."

I wonder how many of us conceive of the Christian life in that way. Many people conceive of Christianity in terms that are certainly lower than those given in the definition. Some people think of Christianity as something that belongs to certain countries. They regard this country, for instance, as a Christian country. Some government officials who regard themselves as Christians, and look on those whom they govern as pagans; they regard themselves as Christians simply because they are Britishers, not because they have had any real experience, or have any real interest in spiritual things.

There are others who conceive of Christianity in terms of infant baptism. If you ask them to give you their reason for calling themselves Christians, they say that when they were infants they were baptized; it was an enactment that took place between the minister and the parents, with the child being, in essence, unconscious, yet they think that enactment somehow made them Christians.

It is a great fallacy to imagine that this view is confined to the Anglican or Roman Catholic churches; it is found among others as well. The enactment of infant baptism has nothing to do with the life of God entering a person's soul. Some people confuse Christianity with being received into the membership of the church. A child reaches an age at which it is felt he ought to be a full member of the church. So he is given a certain amount of instruction and information, and when he can answer all the questions perfectly, he is received into the full communion of the church. But there is no insistence on an experience. Many people have been received into the fellowship of the church on that basis alone. Nothing was said about the life of God in their soul.

Then there are others who describe Christianity in terms of good works, morality, and good behavior. They argue that many people can be received into the full membership of the church on the basis of intellectual knowledge, but whose lives often deny the truth to which they subscribe with their lips.

The Life of God

These are just some of the definitions of the Christian life with which we are familiar today; but I think we must all admit that they fall hopelessly short of John Wesley's favorite definition. They all speak of Christianity in terms of something done, whereas the Scotsman's definition describes it as the life of God in the soul of man. It is to illustrate the truth of that definition that we turn, finally, to the familiar Old Testament incident of the widow and the cruse of oil.

If Christianity is the "life of God," then it is divine in its very essence; and because it is supernatural it is obviously something that man can never arrive at by his own effort. It is a gift, something which has to be received. Lest there be someone who doubts this, let us look at the picture given to us in Scripture. Here is a poor widow in debt with creditors pressing in on her; her friends try to console her and help her meet her creditors, yet their efforts are insufficient. It is a picture of a crisis.

The New Testament is full of this kind of picture. Paul says in First Corinthians, "Though I speak with the tongues of men and of angels, and have not charity, I am become as sounding brass, or a tinkling cymbal" (13:1). It is one thing to preach, Paul is telling us. I may sway great congregations; I may be eloquent; I may speak almost like an angel; but that does not produce life within.

Paul goes on to speak of utterly selfless men who give of their gifts to feed the poor. Surely such men must be right spiritually. Not necessarily, says Paul. Such a man may be devoid of love in his heart. His generosity does not necessarily produce this life that is the essence of Christianity. Even the giving of one's life does not produce this primary fruit of the Spirit called life. It is a miracle, it is a supernatural life, and the highest effort of man can never reach it.

The Mystery of the Christian Life

Not only can a man by his own efforts not produce this kind of life, but also the man who does not possess it cannot even understand it. Let us visit for a moment the village in which the widow from the Second Book of Kings lives. Let us go to the square in the center of the village one morning at about ten o'clock. Let us take a look at a group of people meeting together there. They have met together to discuss the case of the poor widow and are looking anxious and concerned, even hopeless; they feel that nothing can be done.

That is the scene in the morning, but come along to the same spot in the afternoon; there we see the same people again, only this time their faces are animated. They have just heard that the widow has been able to pay her debts, and that she has an abundance to spare. How has it happened? It seemed so utterly hopeless in the morning, but now they are rejoicing with her. They cannot understand it.

That is an Old Testament picture of a New Testament truth. We have another one in the case of Nicodemus and his nighttime interview with our Lord. "Master, I have been watching You," says Nicodemus to Christ. "I have seen your miracles; I have listened to your teaching; and I can see very clearly that you are no ordinary man. I have come to you that I might discover the secret. I am a master in Israel. How can I reach the standard that you have reached?"

"Nicodemus," replies our Lord, "your question betrays you. It is clear that you do not understand the elements of this life of which I speak. What you need is not promotion, but regeneration. You are in the wrong school altogether; you must be born again. This life of God I speak of is more comparable to the wind than anything else; you cannot see the wind—you see only its effect. You bow your head, and allow its gracious influences to exercise themselves on you. It is not to be understood; it is to be accepted."

Paul sets forth this truth in the First Epistle to the Corinthians: "But the natural man receiveth not the things of the Spirit of God: for they are foolishness unto him: neither can he know them, because they are spiritually discerned" (2:14).

Not only can this life of God not be understood by the man who doesn't possess it, but also even the man who does possess it cannot understand it. In the story about the widow, the villagers were surprised when they heard the news but the one who was the most surprised was the woman herself. In my mind I can see her standing there with the pot in her hand, looking with astonishment at the never-failing supply of oil.

Has not Paul said the same thing? "I live, yet not I, but Christ liveth in me" (Gal. 2:20). "I do not understand myself," he says. "I am Saul of Tarsus, and yet I am not." How astonished the Christian himself is when this life of God enters into his soul.

Someone may say, "You have emphasized the divine nature of this life, and you have shown that man of himself has nothing to do with the bestowal of this life, so that really, all one has to do is just sit down and wait for this miraculous life to enter into one's soul." No, I am not saying that. I am not saying that we have nothing at all to do. There is only one actor in the great drama, and that is the Lord Jesus Christ himself. No one can take his place, but we can at least prepare the stage for him.

In her distress the poor widow goes to the prophet and asks his help. "What have you in the house?" he asks. "I've got nothing except a pot of oil," is her reply. "Well, well, that is all right," says the prophet, "as long as you do exactly what I tell you." Then he gives her his instructions. First, she is to go into her secret chamber alone with her boys and herself. The miracle did not take place in the middle of the village, but in the secret chamber. God seldom does his big things in the crowded mart, or in the busy street. If we would enter into this life we must have some kind of secret chamber into which we can retire. In a busy world like this we must have a sanctuary in which we can be alone. It is not enough that we should merely shut out the world; we must also shut in ourselves. Get into that inner room, and lock the door. Get alone with God's Book; spend time dwelling on the things of eternity. The second thing which the prophet instructs the woman to do is to gather together empty vessels to receive the oil. What does that mean for us? I think many of us fail to enjoy the higher blessings of the Christian life simply because we have never expected them. We come to our place of worship on Sunday not actually expecting a blessing; we don't even believe that it is possible. Perhaps we have accepted the teaching of psychology that explains away conversion and the miracle of regeneration. If you do not believe in the possibility of conversion you will never experience it. Gather together your empty vessels. Believe in the fact that this blessing is for you; then go to the service on the tiptoe of expectation. Prepare for the miracle of God's grace; that is your part. Get away from the mindset of the world and look to God for the blessing.

Choosing Much or Little

Finally, the amount of blessing we receive depends entirely on ourselves; if the amount of the blessing depended on God there would literally be no end to it. When the widow tells the prophet that she has nothing but a pot of oil, he tells her, "Go borrow the vessels of *all* thy neighbors" (italics added). Not just one here and there. God is going to work a miracle, therefore, she must get hold of every single vessel she could. God's blessing is an endless, eternal ocean.

Evangelist Dwight L. Moody told how for a number of years he was just a nominal, formal kind of Christian, who felt he lacked this greater blessing. He longed for it, and he prepared himself for it, yet it did not come. Suddenly, one afternoon as he was walking down the street in New York City, the blessing came; it was so overwhelming in its power that Moody felt it would kill him, and he held up his hand and cried, "Stop, Lord!"

I can see now the procession of empty vessels receiving the oil. The woman asks for another vessel and is told that there are no more—"and the oil stayed." While they had the empty vessels to receive it, the oil continued to flow.

What a tragedy it is that so many Christians are content to live as paupers, whereas God intends them to be princes! This mystic experience of the fullness of God was not something just for Paul and the first Christians. It is something that ordinary men and women have received throughout the ages. It is something that is offered to us here today.

2

The Hope of the Christian

And we desire that every one of you do shew the same diligence to the full assurance of hope unto the end: That ye be not slothful, but followers of them who through faith and patience inherit the promises. (Heb. 6:11–12)

In verses eleven and twelve of the sixth chapter of the Book of Hebrews we have what I feel is the center of this great Epistle. Throughout, it is characterized by the extraordinary way in which the writer alternates passages of exhortation with passages of exposition. He is writing to these Hebrew Christians because of the condition in which they found themselves. The writer is concerned about their souls; he is eager to save them from falling away from the grace of the gospel, and to do that he found it necessary not only to give them instruction, but also to rebuke them.

The charge he makes against these people, in effect, is this—that their Christian life has been lacking in balance and in poise. He congratulates them on the fact that in certain respects they have been doing well; but their trouble is that

Preached in the Metropolitan Tabernacle

they have paid too much attention to one side of the Christian faith and have ignored the other side, which is of equal importance. They have done remarkably well on the practical side of Christianity—they've been kind and helpful to one another—but they have been neglecting the intellectual and theological side of the Christian life; they have been negligent in the area of doctrine.

In chapter five the writer depicts Jesus Christ as the great High Priest, after the order of Melchisedec, "Of whom we have many things to say, and hard to be uttered, seeing ye are dull of hearing. . . . and are become such as have need of milk, and not of strong meat" (vv. 11–12). I find myself, says this writer, in a very difficult position owing to the fact that you are dull of hearing. You have neglected the doctrinal and intellectual side of your Christian life. You are not in a fit condition to hear what I have to say. You are in that condition in which you need nothing but milk, whereas what I have to give you is strong meat not suited for babes.

In other words, the real trouble with these Christians was that they had not laid firm hold of that teaching with regard to the ultimate hope of the Christian; they had neglected "the full assurance of hope unto the end."

The Test of Orthodoxy

Now it is because I think that a word like this is not at all inappropriate to the present generation of Christians that I am calling attention to it. The Christian life today tends to be characterized by this same lack of balance. We need to be reminded of that which is central and vital to the Christian faith.

Suppose I put to you the question, What do you consider to be the acid test for the Christian? I can imagine someone answering, "The acid test of the Christian is the test of orthodoxy; the way to prove whether or not someone is a Christian is to question him in regard to his belief. Is he orthodox? Does he believe in God, in the deity of Christ, in the atonement, in the resurrection, and in the person of the Holy Spirit?" We would all agree, of course, that if a man is not orthodox he cannot be a Christian. He must believe in the being of God and in the deity of Christ if he be a Christian. Yet, though essential, orthodoxy really does not provide an acid test of our Christian profession.

I always feel about the test of orthodoxy that it is analogous to those preliminary tests held in connection with various competitions. For instance, when the Eisteddfod (festival of arts) in Wales is held, it is essential that there be some kind of preliminary test. Perhaps some forty to fifty contestants will enter, and as a result of the preliminary test five or six competitors will be selected, and will be the only ones to appear on the platform before the entire audience. The function of the preliminary test is to eliminate a vast majority of the competitors. The test of orthodoxy in connection with the Christian profession is a kind of preliminary test. It is a negative thing; if a man is not orthodox he is not a Christian. I suggest to you that it does not merit the name acid test because it is not sufficiently positive. There are a number of people who are perfectly orthodox in their belief; they have an intellectual apprehension of the truth of the gospel, but their hearts have never been changed.

The Test of Life

I can imagine someone else answering that the acid test for the Christian is the test of behavior—the test of the life. The person will say, "I have known a number of people who were very orthodox in their belief, but whose lives proved very clearly they were not really Christians. To me the real test of the Christian is the way in which a man lives. Does he live a good and clean life? Does he do good to his fellow men? Is he like his Master, going about everywhere doing good?"

What are we to say to such a statement? Once more we have to agree at once that if a man does not live a good life he is not a Christian; that if he does not live a life worthy of the gospel, however orthodox he may be in his belief, he is really not a Christian. The test of life, therefore, is also a very valuable and essential test. But again, we have all of us known a number of people whose lives were above reproach—highly moral people at whom you could never point the finger of scorn. But, nevertheless, a good life alone does not make one a Christian. There are thousands who fall into that error. You will hear a man say, "It doesn't matter whether I attend a place of worship or not; so long as I am a good man, I am a Christian." The New Testament utterly rejects such a notion as an acid test.

The Test of Experience

The third man who answers our question is a very modern man. "I entirely agree," he says, "that orthodoxy is not enough, and that mere morality and good behavior are not sufficient. In my opinion the acid test of the Christian is this: Has he had an experience? Can he say that he has a changed life? Can he say, 'Whereas I was blind, now I see'? Can he testify to the fact that he is a new man, with a new experience in his life?"

What are we to say to this? We agree at once that experience is an essential thing. If a man has not had this experience, whether it be sudden or gradual, he is not a Christian. No man is born into the world a Christian; each individual must be born again to become a Christian. If a man cannot say that there has been a great changeover in his life, he is not a Christian. And yet if we take up the position of saying that experience alone matters, we shall be falling into a very grievous error: the Christian Scientist talks about an experience; you can consult a psychoanalyst, and then talk about an experience; there are the various religious cults that can furnish you with an experience.

My own answer to my question is that the acid test for the Christian is his attitude toward the question of the Christian hope. Here is something that is central, and covers the entire ground. You will find it everywhere in the New Testament. One of the last things Jesus said to his disciples was, "I go to prepare a place for you. And if I go and prepare a place for you I will come again and receive you unto myself." He left them with that thought. Paul also speaks of hope. "That ye may know what is the hope of his calling," he wrote to the Ephesians. Peter is called the apostle of hope. If you read through the first chapter of his Epistle you will be amazed at the number of times he uses the word. And hope is, of course, central and vital in the Epistles of John and in the Book of the Revelation.

What Is the Christian Hope?

If our attitude toward the Christian hope is the test of our profession, it becomes vitally important that we know exactly what it is. Let me share with you, first of all, what it is not, as there is much confusion about this subject. Many people seem to regard the Christian hope as merely a matter of temperament; the man who has the Christian hope is seen as a man who is an optimist—a genial, cheerful kind of man, always smiling. But we are not all born with such a temperament. This Christian hope is not merely a matter of temperament or a question of optimistic philosophy. The gospel of Christ faces life in a realistic manner. It never comforts people by telling them to turn their backs on the world, or by intoxicating them with wonderful phrases.

Well then, what is this Christian hope? I often meet people who seem to think that hope is just the opposite of certainty and assurance. If you ask them whether they have the assurance of salvation, they reply that they are not sure—they *hope* they are saved.

According to these people, hope is the antithesis of assurance. But our text proves how ridiculous such a conception is. The writer exhorts those to whom he is writing to "show the same diligence to the full assurance of hope unto the end." Hope does not mean uncertainty. Indeed, according to the New Testament, there is nothing quite as certain as this hope that is set before us; the doctrine of this hope tells us that our salvation is something that is mainly future. In this life we merely receive the first installment of our salvation, what Paul calls "the earnest of our inheritance." Salvation is something that is mainly future. There is a great estate awaiting us. We have not entered into it yet, but we have been given the title deeds. There is laid up for us in Christ a glorious possession: ". . . Eye hath not seen, nor ear heard . . . the things which God hath prepared for them that love him" (1 Cor. 2:9). That is, in its essence, the New Testament doctrine of this Christian hope—that we have merely received the installment, the first fruits, but that the full salvation itself is in the future. We are the children of God, therefore heirs, and joint heirs with Christ. That is the great hope that is set before us. And the acid test of our profession is our grasp of that doctrine. Is that central in our lives?

If a man believes in this doctrine, he must be orthodox; he must believe in the deity of Christ, in his atonement and resurrection. What is there that can really comfort and encourage men in a world such as this, save this doctrine of the blessed hope? These people to whom the Epistle was addressed were Jews who had become Christians. They had been told about the atoning death and resurrection of Jesus of Nazareth and that he was coming back again; they had given up their old Jewish practices and had given themselves to him. But as the years passed by, and as Christ did not return, these people began to wonder whether they had not made a mistake after all. In the meantime, they were being persecuted by the Jews, the Romans, and others, and they were beginning to waver in their belief. Then someone writes this Epistle to them, saying, "You have never quite grasped the doctrine: that is why you are contemplating going back."

We were never told that we would have an easy time
here. Our salvation is mainly future. The world may kill us,
but it can never rob us of our hope. There is no real comfort
and consolation in this world apart from that hope.

What do you fall back on when things go wrong—when
you face disappointments in business; when you are laid
aside by illness? When you face death, what do you rest on?
Is it not this glorious hope that he is coming again, and that
we shall one day be with him? It is our one source of
comfort and consolation, as we face the trials and tribulations of this world.

In addition, this doctrine of the Christian hope is really
the only adequate incentive to Christian living. Let me put it
to you in this way: If I take up the position of saying that I
am orthodox, and that orthodoxy is the acid test of the
Christian hope, then I can rest on my oars; I have nothing
further to do, and I will probably backslide. Likewise, the
man who emphasizes the value of his experience will always
look back to that experience; and while he is looking back he
cannot be traveling forward. I often meet people who tell me
of some religious experience they have had. But what has
been happening in the meantime? Such people are ever
looking back to that first experience.

The doctrine of the blessed hope is the only incentive to
true Christian living. The day is coming when I shall see
Christ face to face. When I think of that estate, which I shall
one day enter, when I try to conceive of the glory and
wonder of salvation, I press forward. The hope that is set
before me inspires me to diligence in my Christian life.

I need to remember that there is a day coming when I
shall appear before the judgment seat of Christ to give an
account of the deeds done in the body. With some who have
accepted this Christian doctrine there is a tendency to
indolence and lethargy. One day we shall see him as he is,
and I fear that only then will we realize what our salvation
has cost him. When we shall look into his blessed face, when

we see the imprint of the nails in his hands and feet—we shall feel a sense of shame for all our slackness.

Perhaps someone is saying, "That is all very well; but how can I be perfectly certain that all that you are saying is true? How can I really make certain of this hope?" The author of Hebrews answers that question in the remainder of the chapter. If you want to be certain, he says, fall back on your own history. He tells the story of Abraham who hoped against hope. He believed the word of God though there was nothing to show for it. The Christian hope is as certain as this—the character of God is behind it: "Which hope we have as an anchor of the soul, both sure and stedfast, and which entereth into that within the veil" (Heb. 6:19). Christ tore asunder the bands of death, he rose triumphant from the grave, he entered in to heaven; there we have our confidence. And he will come again and receive us unto himself. So I beseech you, "show the same diligence to the full assurance of hope unto the end."

3

True Christian Discipleship

From that time many of his disciples went back, and walked no more with him. Then said Jesus unto the twelve, Will ye also go away? Then Simon Peter answered him, Lord, to whom shall we go? thou hast the words of eternal life. (John 6:66–68)

I feel it is always an interesting and profitable subject to try to decide which is the more dangerous position for a man to be in—either to state openly and avowedly that he is not at all interested in Christ and religion, or to follow Christ for the wrong and for the false reason. I know every theologian in this congregation will be led to say at once that, ultimately, there is no difference between these two men—the one who follows Christ for the wrong and false reason is as much outside the kingdom as the man who makes no pretense to follow Christ at all. That is perfectly true. But I do think there is an important distinction between the two when you regard things merely from the human standpoint. For the difficulty with the man who follows Christ for a wrong or false reason is that he not

Preached in Westminster Church, Buckingham Gate

23

only deludes himself, but he also deludes the church. When you are confronted by one who says he does not believe in Christ, then you know exactly what to say and what to do with him. When a man presents himself as a religious person, the church tends to take him for granted; to question him would be considered an insult. The church assumes that because he acknowledges himself to be a religious man, therefore, he is a Christian. One of the most dangerous places for such a man to be in is the church of the living God.

I am not at all sure but that one explanation for the present state of the church is to be found at just that point: she has been far too ready to associate church membership with true discipleship, and to assume that all who join the church are really following Christ. I know the church may have a very good motive for doing so. She has felt it a very good thing for people to be within the home of the church so that she may protect them from the temptations of the world. Taking it for granted that these people are truly Christians, the church addresses to them messages that are not of much value to those lacking the essence of the faith.

Thus, I say that the church can be a very dangerous place. Because these people are in the church it may be that they will never be directly addressed by some of the fundamental questions that all true Christians must be able to answer.

There is a real danger of our assuming that we are Christians for wrong reasons, and I do not hesitate to say that it is a very real and great danger. Were you to ask me to substantiate those adjectives I could do so very easily from the pages of the New Testament itself.

Christians for the Wrong Reasons

As you read the story of the life of our Lord in the Gospels, there is, surely, nothing quite so striking as the way he seemed to live almost in terror lest men and women should come after him for the wrong reason. You will find him constantly asking them whether they are following him for the right reason. He was extremely concerned lest he should attract those who had not really laid hold of the right and true things.

Some people will tell you that when Christ was deserted by his friends at the end of his life, he was taken by surprise, having never anticipated such desertion. But this is false to the New Testament picture that we have of him. Our Lord was aware of this possibility from the very beginning. He actually predicted it. He constantly took great pains to question his followers, because he knew for certain what was ultimately going to take place. We all remember those incredible words that he used at the end of the Sermon on the Mount: "Many will say to me in that day, Lord, Lord, have we not prophesied in thy name? and in thy name have cast out devils? and in thy name done many wonderful works? And then will I profess unto them, I never knew you: depart from me . . ." (Matt. 7:22–23). Such people thought that everything was all right, and in that day they will discover that everything was all wrong.

We remember too the parable of the house built on the rock and the house built on the sand: "Take heed now ye hear," says our Lord. "Examine yourselves: sift yourselves."

Then there is the parable of the sower in which our Lord seems to say that of those who go after him only some 25 percent have really grasped the truth.

I would remind you also of the parable of the dragnet, in which there were a number of fish, some good and some bad, pointing to the great division of the people.

But perhaps the most perfect illustration of this principle is found in one of the three pictures at the end of the ninth chapter of Luke's Gospel. A young man came running to Jesus and said, "Lord, I will follow thee whithersoever thou goest" (v. 57). In other words, "I do not know about these other people, but as for me, I am all out." Surely, someone will say, that is the kind of man that the church of God is looking for at the present time; surely our Lord must have received him with open arms. But it was to that man that Jesus said, "Foxes have holes, and birds of the air have nests: but the Son of man hath not where to lay his head" (v. 58). Christ turns to this zealot, and says, in essence, "You are full of zeal and enthusiasm and ecstasy, but wait a moment. Do you realize exactly what it may mean to follow me?"

Following Christ means ostracism; it means giving up the things that you may value most in life. Make certain you know exactly what Christian discipleship means. As you read the Gospels you will find that our Lord is constantly careful to warn people of the possibility of going after him for the wrong reason. Those who wrote the Epistles reiterated the same message in their instructions to the early Christians.

Those Who Remained

Should we not examine ourselves, asking whether we are following him for the right or the wrong reason? Why *are* we following him? What is the precise meaning and significance that we attach to our own church membership? This last question I would like to consider in the light of our text.

The Evangelist writes: "From that time many of his disciples went back." On the other hand, the Twelve remained. Many returned; a few remained. Many had gone after Jesus for the wrong reason; the few had gone after him for the right and true reason. Let us look at some of the false reasons men have for following Christ.

There were many who went after our Lord simply because they saw the crowds surrounding him. So too, there are people today who become attached to the church for the simple reason that many other people are doing the same thing. You can see quite clearly in the New Testament—as well as in church history—that there is a good deal of mob psychology. There are people who are always ready to join a crowd, who are always fascinated by what everybody else is doing.

Some people are in the church for the simple reason that they have been taken there, or have seen others going there. They have never asked themselves the question, "*Why* am I in the church?" It just seems to be the right thing for them to do: their parents and their grandparents did it, it's a tradition in their town, others are doing it. They are merely being carried down the stream. God forbid that any of us should be in the church thoughtlessly, never having actually faced the question of true membership and what it involves.

Another false reason for following Christ is indicated by our Lord in John 6:26. "Jesus answered them, and said, Verily, verily, I say unto you, Ye seek me, not because ye saw the miracles, but because ye did eat of the loaves, and were filled." What does he mean? Jesus was suggesting that these people had a purely mercenary and materialistic reason for going after him. They seemed to be worshiping him, but they weren't really interested in the supernatural. Why did they follow him? Because they had received from him that which had appealed to them—the loaves. They were anxious to be given food, and for that selfish reason went after him.

I don't know that this is a very common reason why people join the church, but it is tragic that men attach themselves to the church because it gives them position or status or power or influence. Alas, men have even joined the church because it helped their business or profession; they have made use of the church to further personal interests and desires. These are the people who go after Christ because they are anxious to eat of the loaves and be filled.

(Perhaps we ought to place in this category those who go after Christ simply because they are interested in the doctrine of the forgiveness of sins—they do not want to suffer eternal punishment. Christ announces pardon for sin, and they go after him, not because they desire holiness, or because they really love him, but because they fear hell.

These are the people who use the cross of Christ as a cloak
to cover their sins. They follow Christ solely to serve their
own ends, and not because he is the Son of God, and the
Savior of the world.)

"Because of the Miracles"

There is another interesting type of person whom we
meet frequently in the pages of the New Testament. This
person is described in verse 2: "And a great multitude
followed him, because they saw his miracles which he did
on them that were diseased." We get another look at the
same type of person in the second chapter of John. "Now
when he was in Jerusalem at the passover, in the feast day,
many believed in his name, when they saw the miracles
which he did" (v. 23).

This person is concerned with the externals of religion
and tends to be rather common at the present time. These
are the people who are interested in the phenomena of
religion rather than by the truth of religion; they go after
Jesus because they see the miracles that he does. Christ's
miraculous power appeals to them. If there is a display of
supernatural power, they are always there.

Our Lord Jesus Christ performed many miracles, and he
did so deliberately. His object and purpose in performing
them was to manifest his power. Yet the interesting thing is
this: he does not commit himself to those who are more
interested in the miracles than in the man, to those who are
more interested in the phenomena than in the power. Jesus
Christ, by the grace of God, still performs miracles in this
sinful world, and still changes the lives of men. There are still
glorious phenomena in connection with the kingdom of God
in Christ Jesus. But Christ did not come to earth merely to
work miracles, to do mighty deeds, and so to manifest his
power. He did not come even to change our lives. He came
primarily to gather to himself a peculiar people zealous for
good works. He came to reconcile men to God, and to bring

us to a knowledge of the truth. We must beware of following him simply because we are more interested in the phenomena that in the truth itself.

The final group is found in verses 14 and 15, where we read, "Then those men, when they had seen the miracle that Jesus did, said, This is of a truth that prophet that should come into the world. When Jesus therefore perceived that they would come and take him by force, to make him a king, he departed again into a mountain himself alone." Here we have an interesting group of people who follow him because they completely and entirely misunderstand him and his message. What was the miracle that they had seen? It was the feeding of the five thousand. These people, according to the context, had been following our Lord for a number of days, perhaps weeks. They had listened to him, but it was only when they saw the miracle that they said, "This is the Messiah; this is the Prophet that was to come." Then they conspired together and agreed that they must approach him, and take him by force to Jerusalem to make him a king. But Jesus observed their intention, and withdrew himself to a mountain.

These Jews had a political conception of the kingdom of heaven. They conceived of the Messiah as a political liberator, one who would deliver them from Roman bondage, and establish himself king in Jerusalem where he would reign over their enemies, and over the whole world. These men approached Jesus with that idea in their minds but he resisted them, and ultimately they became members of that company that went from him.

How many there are still who think of Jesus as a political agitator or social reformer. How many there are who think of the kingdom of heaven as being primarily secular and political. How many there are who think that one of the main functions of the church is to deal with the social condition of the world, to take its place in various departments and walks of human life, and to decide great questions in regard to industry and politics and international affairs. How many there are still who think of Christ as a social reformer, as a political agitator. And how many others there are who think of him rather as the pale Galilean who holds men aloof, as too sensitive even to touch the world. Some there are who think of him as the great artist, or the great ascetic, or the incomparable philosopher. There are those who approach his Book as if it were merely a collection of literary gems. If we took out of the church all these various groups, I wonder how many people we would have left. I fear that the "many" would assume an alarming proportion.

The Testing of a Disciple

I make no apology in asking you, Do you follow Christ? Have you faced this question? Have you stood face to face with these possibilities? The people I have mentioned were going after Christ. They had been with him for days; they called themselves his disciples. Then, we read, many of them walked no more with him. Why have *we* gone after him? Have we the right reasons, or are we guilty of one of these false reasons?

What is the true reason for following Christ? The answer is to be found in those great words of Simon Peter. "Then said Jesus unto the twelve, Will ye also go away? Then Simon Peter answered him, Lord, to whom shall we go? thou hast the words of eternal life. And we believe and are sure that thou art that Christ, the Son of the living God" (John 6:67–69).

Now we can be very happy about this answer, for, as the context shows us, the Lord tested the faith of the Twelve. The many were going back. "There they go; you see them," says our Lord. "They have heard the same sermons that you have; they have seen the same miracles; you and they are in exactly the same position. Do you want to go with them? Have you been following me for the same reason that they have? For, if you have, then I prefer not to have you. Will you also go away?'' And Simon Peter answers with confidence and certainty. In his words is the irreducible minimum of true Christian discipleship. What do they mean, these words of Peter? We must break them up for analysis.

"Lord, to whom shall we go?'' Peter says. Should we interpret that sentence emotionally? Did Peter turn to our Lord and say "We have been having such a wonderful time together that life would be impossible without you''? Was it a statement of emotional attachment? Yes, it was that, and also very much more. It was a profound definition of faith. Peter asked "To whom shall we go?'' because he realized he could not save himself. He had long since realized his own helpless condition. He had been looking for someone outside himself for salvation. But he didn't merely admit that he could not save himself. He also stated very definitely his absolute certainty that only Christ could save him.

"I cannot save myself,'' says Peter, "and no other man can save me.'' There is always this negative statement in the basic Christian confession. To what and to whom are we pinning our faith? The man who has any conceivable alternative to Christ is not a Christian.

What do we hold on to as we think of death and eternity? Are we still trusting in that delusion of a world that is supposed to be advancing and developing? Are we still fondly imagining that mere intellectual attainments can fit us for heaven?

"I cannot save myself,'' says Peter. "Man cannot save me. The world cannot save me. But I believe that you can.'' And he gives his reason: "Thou art the Christ, the Son of the living God. Thou hast the words of eternal life.'' In the face of Jesus Christ Peter saw God.

Have you ever taken your stand with Simon Peter? Have you ever realized your own bankruptcy and sinfulness? And have you said to Christ, "Thou must save, and thou alone?'' Peter is not content merely with avowing that Christ is the Son of the living God. He says, "We cannot leave you, for thou hast the words of eternal life.''

The other people had gone after Christ; they had listened to his sermons; they had appreciated his miracles. Then our Lord, in one of his sermons, compared himself with the manna that came down from heaven, and went on to say that he was the living bread, and that unless men would eat of his flesh they could never have eternal life. And many of his disciples, when they heard this, said, "This is a hard saying." Ultimately they went back because of those words. Jesus spoke of men eating his flesh, and drinking his blood, and made that the postulate of eternal life. "How can that be?" the people asked, offended. But Peter responds: "I do not understand it all, but I believe it."

My friends, it is not enough that we should ascribe deity to Jesus of Nazareth. It is not enough that we should believe in his miracles. We only really and truly follow him when we believe that he ultimately achieves our salvation through his broken body and his shed blood.

"I do not understand the doctrine of the atonement," you say. "I cannot fathom it; it seems mysterious, almost immoral." I am not asking you to understand it all. Simon Peter did not understand it, but he accepted it, and he committed his life to Christ.

Jesus Christ offers himself to us crucified, bruised by the stripes that we deserved as one, who not only delivers us from the guilt of our past sin, but who delivers us from the very power and pollution of sin. He stands before us and says, "Take of me. Will ye also go away?"

Thousands are going away from him. The country and the world are becoming increasingly irreligious. Man in his intellectual pride is rejecting the Word of God. "Will ye also go away?" Shall we not all together turn to him, and with Simon Peter say, "Lord, to whom shall we go? Thou hast the words of eternal life. And we believe and are sure that thou art that Christ, the Son of the living God"?

4

The Problem of Suffering

*Furthermore we have had fathers of our flesh which
corrected us, and we gave them reverence: shall we
not much rather be in subjection unto the Father of
spirits, and live? For they verily for a few days chastened us after their own pleasure; but he for our
profit, that we might be partakers of his holiness.*
(Heb. 12:9–10)

It is abundantly clear from the twelfth chapter of
the Book of Hebrews that the author of this Epistle is dealing
with the whole problem of suffering, especially in connection with the Christian life. Indeed, that was his reason for
writing the Epistle. The Christians to whom he was writing
had become despondent not only because the Lord's return
had not taken place, but also because they were being
persecuted; these things did not quite tally with their conception of the Christian faith.

I imagine that, in the final analysis, it is this sense of
disappointment, this feeling that the gospel is not doing
what it promised, that causes the greatest trouble to so
many. If we were to take a census of those who have turned

Preached in Westminster Chapel

away from organized Christianity in this century, we would probably find that a high percentage of them left because they felt they were undergoing trials and difficulties which they could not reconcile with the teaching of the New Testament—especially in regard to the love of God.

There were many people during World War I who faced this question. They could not reconcile a God of love with the things that were happening in the world—and to them personally. Young men of noble character were taken away while other men living worldy and sinful lives were allowed to live—they felt that these things could not be reconciled with the idea of a God of love. As a result many of them turned their backs on Christianity.

Many a godly man has been overwhelmed by financial problems and difficulties, while the ungodly man flourishes. The godly man is unable to reconcile it with what he reads in the New Testament.

There are also those who are constantly in a state of ill health; others have had dear ones taken from them, sometimes at an early age.

Men and women experience these trials and tribulations, and they come to the conclusion that though the gospel makes great and glorious promises, God somehow fails to keep them. While not all who have turned away from Christianity for such reasons, many who remain loyal to the church have similar feelings and doubts; it is to these people that I address my remarks, holding before them the tenth verse of the twelfth chapter of Hebrews: "For they verily for a few days chastened us after their own pleasure; but he for our profit, that we might be partakers of his holiness."

What is the New Testament's reply to situations such as those mentioned above? What answer does the gospel give to those who feel that life's circumstances seem to deny the promises of Christianity?

Under the Common Law

We must recognize first of all that an answer can be given to these people merely on the grounds of ordinary human reasoning. Often Christians allow themselves to become depressed because they do not apply ordinary common sense to the situation with which they are confronted. In terms of ordinary human reasoning the answer seems to be that these troublesome things of life are things that happen to us quite apart from Christianity altogether. They are the "accidents" of life and they take place in the lives of men and women whether or not they are Christians. Though the Christian is not *of* this world, he is *in* this world, and is still subject to the ordinary laws that govern it. The Christian is still a citizen of the country to which he belongs, and the things that happen to that country will affect him also. Christians are not the only people who suffer loss. They are not the only ones who have difficulties in business. There are times when we are like the author of Psalm 73 thinking these things happen only to godly people. If you take the trouble to make a dispassionate analysis of the bad things that take place, I think you will find that Christian people are afflicted in precisely the same way as are other people.

Another deduction that can be drawn, quite apart from the revelation of Scripture is that the mere reading of secular history seems to show that Christians are not promised magical lives. Curiously, we all seem to harbor that strange notion that the Christian life is a life that, once entered is lived out happily ever after—that Christianity offers one a charmed life in which one is miraculously protected, able to recline in ease and happiness for the rest of his days. But history proves such a notion utterly and entirely wrong; in fact, it seems to teach exactly the opposite—that Christians should expect *more* trouble than other people. We read, for instance, of Christians being persecuted because of their faith. Far from being a charmed life, the Christian life through history has seemed to prove true the words of Paul to the Philippians: "For unto you it is given in the behalf of Christ, not only to believe on him, but also to suffer for his sake" (1:29). Instead of applying common sense to our situation, we become stunned by our difficulties and problems, and begin complaining before we have even thought of the situation in ordinary human terms.

The "Indirectness" of the Bible

We need to realize that the New Testament does not provide a precise and exact answer to every problem we happen to be confronting. Christians seem to think that it should supply an immediate answer but the New Testament doesn't claim to do that; it provides general principles that will cover any problem that can ever be settled.

In addition, the New Testament never deals with such matters directly, but always indirectly. This Book doesn't necessarily administer immediate comfort. Many people seem to regard it as though it were some kind of a drug, something to take when they are troubled with some problem, and which immediately makes them feel better. They expect immediate results. (There is a danger that people may come to church for the same reason—that they may be made to feel better. Surely we come to worship God, and not that we might forget our problems.) I have met those who claim that the best cure for insomnia is to read the Psalms. The magnificence of the poetry, the cadence and lilt of the words somehow or other soothes and comforts a person and soon he drops off to sleep. That is an abuse of the Bible. That is to use the Bible directly rather than indirectly—to use it as a kind of drug, as a sleeping pill, an intoxicant.

How prone we are to confuse the ornate and outward things with the spiritual. You never find the writers of the Epistles merely administering comfort. The New Testament pays us a great compliment by giving us its comfort in terms of doctrine. The writer of Hebrews doesn't say to his readers,

"You are a wonderful people, and you are really doing
magnificently. If you will only hold on, everything will turn
out all right in the end." No, he reprimands them, he warns
them, he seems to deal with them very harshly. It all seems
very strange to our modern ears, to those who desire
immediate and direct comfort. But this is the very glory of
the New Testament; it gives us doctrine, it regards us as
intelligent human beings. It says, "Stand on your feet for a
moment. Here is doctrine. Work it out for yourself." And
that is precisely what the writer does in verse 10: he is
reasoning; he is arguing; he is putting the case to them. It is
not a direct comfort, but an indirect comfort.

The Christian Postulate

He tells them that they must start with a postulate of
which they are absolutely certain. Now that, of course, is
the only way to face the problem. A scientist engaged in
research work will always start from the known and proceed
to the unknown. You will never find a good scientist
immediately facing the problem of the unknown. He begins
with a foundation; he lays down something of which he is
absolutely certain.

Now the writer of Hebrews tells his readers that they
must do exactly the same thing with the problems of the
Christian life—they must start with a postulate of which
they are absolutely certain. I am confronted with a problem.
How am I to meet it? I must begin with something of which
I am certain: God is my Father, and, in Jesus Christ, God is
love. Whatever may be happening to me, I can be certain of
that much. In Hebrews we are given that great gallery of the
saints, and are reminded of God's dealing with his people
through the ages. We see him sending them prophets, kings,
and judges, and finally, in the fullness of time, his own Son,
causing him to live in a world like this. We see God not
sparing his only Son, but delivering him up for us all. We see
that the God who does that is our Father, and a God of love,

and for the moment, I do not care what is happening to me; for the moment, I am not concerned with my problem. I start with a foundation on which I can risk everything: God is love; He forgave us even while we were enemies. That is my postulate.

How am I to connect this postulate with my problem? How am I to reconcile the God of love with the things that are happening to me? To begin, let me say that God, as our Father, is much more concerned about our holiness than about our happiness. This is the very essence of the whole question. We like to think of God as our Father, but we forget that Jesus when he prayed, addressed him as *Holy* Father. Let us remember that God is holy and doesn't see things as we do—just *because* he is holy.

Our standards of life tend toward happiness. We desire to have everything in just our own way, according to our own ideas; when something happens that causes us grief or trouble, we immediately begin doubting the love of God. We forget that we are sinful, and that God is holy. God's desire is that we should be holy as he himself is holy. The moment we begin to think along those lines we realize that, although we are Christians, we are nevertheless still in the flesh; there is still the old nature within us, and, desiring certain external comforts, we are all prone to settle down to enjoy life. But there is the danger that we will lie down again in sin, instead of pressing on toward that glorious heritage which God has prepared for us. As our Father, God desires that which is best for us. The author of Hebrews uses the analogy of the human parent, and how perfect an illustration it is. Take, for instance, the boy who thinks his father is unfair to him for not allowing him to do what another boy's father allows him to do. He wishes the other boy's father were his father. He does not understand. His father, of course, has his son's better interests at heart; because he is determined that his boy shall arrive at a particular goal, he prohibits certain things, and enforces certain other things. When we reach heaven we shall be able to see more clearly the loving hand of God in the things which now perplex us. We shall then see how God had to get rid of those angles and rough corners in our character, how he had to stand between us and certain forms of happiness to draw us nearer to himself.

The other point the writer makes is that in the divine purpose, this world is merely a kind of preparatory school. The thought that runs through the Epistle to the Hebrews is that here on earth we have no continuing city; we seek one in the world to come. That is the difficulty. We persist in living as if this were the only life and the only world. We go on making our plans solely for time and we forget eternity. Yet, according to Hebrews this world is nothing but a preparatory school; death is the great matriculation; we look forward to entering the great everlasting university itself. The present time is a time of pilgrimage. This is not really our home. This phantom world is but a brief passing life; we are passing on to eternity, to God, to everlasting peace. If only we could view this life in that way it would transform our characters and our ideas, and help solve our problems. We are like the school boy who would like to evade certain things, and run away from problems and tests. But we thank God that because he has a larger interest in us and knows what is for our good, he puts us through the disciplines of life—he makes us learn the multiplication table; we are made to struggle with the elements of grammar. Many things that are trials to us are essential that one day we may be found without spot or wrinkle. God is our loving Father, and as such his ambition for us is that we should be holy even as he is holy. And here in this preparatory school called life he is teaching and training us that ultimately we may be with him, enjoying the pleasures of eternity.

God grant that, as we meet our problems and trials, we may reason out the case, so that finally we may be able to rejoice even in tribulation because it has brought us nearer to God.

5

The Irreligion of
Self-Content

*Then the five men departed, and came to Laish, and
saw the people that were therein, how they dwelt
careless, after the manner of the Zidonians, quiet
and secure. . . . (Judg. 18:7)*

Chapter eighteen of Judges provides us with
one of those great Old Testament stories worthy of consideration in and of itself. What appeals to me most about this
story is its modernity: it seems to be almost an exact
commentary on the times in which we live.

The story tells of a number of Zidonians who decided to
leave their own country to look for a suitable spot in which
to form a colony. Exactly what prompted them is not
certain. They may have wanted to avoid responsibilities such
as taxation or the defense of their city and district (Zidon),
or perhaps they wished to avoid overcrowding in their
homeland. Reading between the lines, however, I believe
their reason for moving may have been a spirit of laziness—
perhaps they were eager to find a land that was more fruitful

Preached in Westminster Chapel

and would give them larger returns for a minimum amount of labor.

After a little trouble they found a spot that suited them perfectly, and there they settled. We are told that "they dwelt careless, after the manner of the Zidonians, quiet and secure" (v. 7). There was also "no magistrate in the land." In other words, they were a peaceable and peace-loving people. They did not want to interfere with anybody else and they were careless in the matter of defending themselves against possible attacks from the outside. Spies appeared in the land, but they took no notice. They never intended to attack anybody, and it did not occur to them that they would be the subject of attack.

Another thing we are told about the Zidonians is that they were far from those from whom they had separated, and also "had no business with any man" (v. 7). When they left their homeland they cut themselves off completely. They had no dealings with their brethren, and apparently no dealings with anybody else. They seemed to be entirely self-supporting; they were a self-contained unit, living this apparently idyllic life.

And they would have continued in that same manner had not the Danites found themselves in certain difficulties. Desiring room for expansion, they sent out five spies to look for suitable land. The spies entered the land in which these Zidonian colonists dwelt. They saw that it was just what they wanted and went back to the main company of Danites and reported, whereupon six hundred men, fully armed, immediately gathered together and descended upon this colony and with extreme ease killed every single member of it. There was no deliverer because it was far from Zidon, and they "had no business with any man." In a few moments they were overwhelmed and utterly defeated, and their land passed into the hands of the Danites.

Surely I need take very little time in pointing out what a perfect picture we have in this passage, not only of the general situation of the world today, but especially of the religious situation. Tempting as it is to regard this text in the first of these aspects, I shall try to confine my consideration to the second. For, finally and fundamentally, it is the religious situation that matters supremely.

Various Forms of Irreligion

We are all of us in danger of forgetting that irreligion can take many forms. We are constantly tempted to regard irreligion and antagonism toward God as something which, of necessity, falls into certain classes or groups. If we may venture to criticize our immediate forefathers at the end of the last century I would suggest that that was their cardinal error. They identified sin with certain particular sins. The result was that we had all sorts of organizations rising up to fight this, that, and the other sin. They failed to realize that while they were fighting particular sins, the people in general were suffering from a condition which was infinitely more serious—a central godlessness. There was a tendency to equate Christianity with mere temperance or abstinence from certain forms of vice, and that is perhaps still a danger.

Of course when we see a land like Russia prohibiting men from worshiping God, we say that that is irreligion. When we see faithful pastors thrown into concentration camps in Germany, and Christians exhorted to accept a new religion which worships race or ancient myths, we say at once that that is godlessness. When we read the writings of the Rationalist Press Association we are perfectly clear that that is against God and is irreligion. But we are not always awake to another type of irreligion and godlessness, which I would call the Zidonian type.

I suggest that there are large numbers of people in this country and in every country who are strangely similar to the Zidonian colonists in the matter of religion. Here is their story: They were brought up in a religious home and atmosphere. They heard about the Bible and its truths when they were children. They were taught to pray to God, they were taught that Jesus of Nazareth was the Son of God who had come to bring a miraculous salvation, and that they should live a certain kind of life, avoid certain things, and do certain other things. Religion was in a sense popular toward the end of the last century. Places of worship were more or less full throughout the land. There was a definite religious tradition. That was the atmosphere in which people were brought up. Alas! How many thousands, like the Zidonian colonists, have wandered away from that life and have formed a little life of their own and are living an existence which has been mapped out entirely by themselves and according to their own ideas. God no longer counts supreme in their lives. To all intents and purposes they are godless and irreligious. Christianity has not been central in their existence. They have been leading a life of their own, according to their own plan.

Our Modern Zidonians

It is erroneous to imagine that modern Zidonians criticize religion and God in words. We do not find the Zidonians of old criticizing the homeland from which they had come; they just said nothing at all about it. When a man denounces religion in speech or writing we recognize that such a man is anti-God and anti-religious. But the vast majority of people in this country are not guilty of that at all, but rather of having forgotten God altogether. They do not speak against him; they just go on living as if he did not exist. It is not a question of actively speaking and working and organizing against religion.

Again, the religious application of this story is a little more subtle than the story itself. In the case of the biblical Zidonians, they physically left their homeland and went to another. But in the religious application it is not essential that a man cease attending a place of worship. He may still attend and yet, faced with a practical test, be godless and irreligious. God is not central in his life; his life is not based on the dictates of God and his holy law.

What can we say about the Zidonian people in Judges? On the surface there is almost nothing one can say against them. They appear to be nice people. They do not quarrel with one another. They have no need of a magistrate. All they seem to desire is to be left alone.

Modern Zidonians, in comparison, have no objection to religion as long as it talks generalities. They do not like a religion that comes into their daily lives and condemns sin and calls on them to take up a cross. Their main desire is just to be left alone to live their own lives.

The Selfishness of Indifference

What are we to say of such people? The first thing I would say is that their lives are exceedingly selfish. That seems abundantly clear in the case of the Zidonians. They had left their homeland and gone to another place to settle. They had no trade with anyone at all. They wanted to live their lives in their own way. Some may argue that this is not of necessity selfish. Some people think selfishness must be always aggressive. But there is a passive form of selfishness as well as an active one. Selfishness does not always covet what belongs to another. It may show itself in lack of concern for another.

Is that not the appalling truth about this world of ours? Has this not been true even internationally? Has there not been a tendency on the part of nations to say, "It doesn't matter what happens to others so long as we are all right?" Has there not been rampant a nationalism which has said, "Let us live our own lives; let us be isolated; let us fend for ourselves"? Has that not been the great trouble since the last war?

Listen to men's conversations. They are talking about a "good time," by which they mean the maximum of pleasure and enjoyment, and the minimum of work. How little we hear about duty and honor and responsibility. Every man is out for himself. Every man wants comfort and ease. The common phrase has been "to settle down in life," to enjoy ourselves in a detached sort of way from everybody else. Everyone for himself. Has there not been a tendency to contract out of life, to live our own lives in our own little circle? What is the cause of this?

The cause of all this, as I have already suggested, is departure from God, for God tells us that we are to love our neighbor even as ourselves. The Bible, from beginning to end, in the Old Testament and in the New, tells us that we are not to go out and live life in our own way. The Bible tells us that we own nothing of ourselves, that we are just stewards, that God owns everything. The Bible says to a man, Seek ye first the kingdom of God, and all these things shall be added unto you. It tells us not to put a circle round ourselves but to deny ourselves and go out for Christ, bearing his reproach. That is the teaching of the Bible—the selfless life, the life lived for God and under God.

When you read the stories of the saints, do you not find as their supreme virtue a lack of selfishness, a lack of concern for themselves? But ever since the war we have not liked a doctrine like that. It has disturbed us. We have wanted to "settle down" in life. It is this departure from God and his call that has made man so selfish. Compare the typical modern man—with his view of how life should be lived—with one of the great saints. What a contrast! Compare the modern man—with his circumscribed life—with Jesus of Nazareth giving his life for a world that had rejected him. Oh, the selfishness of the godless life that goes away and tries to live to itself in its own godless sphere!

The Small and Shortsighted Life

How shortsighted this view of life is! These Zidonian colonists had left their homeland and settled in another country, and everything was going perfectly. There they were, enjoying themselves to their heart's content. They took no precautions to defend their country against attack. They went on from day to day, hoping present conditions would continue. They were perfectly happy, but it was a happiness based on their failure to analyze their position. If only they had envisaged the possibilities they would have seen what was likely to happen. They were happy sitting on a volcano because it was not erupting at the moment. Then five men came into their land followed by six hundred men armed to the teeth who swept these colonists off the earth.

Need I apply the message? The characteristic of this life is its carelessness. Shall I put it in the form of questions? What kind of life have you been living? Have you been living this careless life? Have you envisaged all the possibilities? Have you considered the eventualities? Have you gone forward in your mind and faced the absolute certainties? Or have you just been living from day to day and hour to hour saying, "Why go out to meet your troubles?" Have you got your defenses in order, your reserves ready, your lines of communication prepared? Have you someone to whom you can turn in your hour of need?

"Why, no," you say, "But everything is all right at the moment!" I am just here to remind you that the five spies have already entered the land. They have gone back to report to the main army. What would you feel like if you lost your occupation, if you lost someone who is dearer to you than life? What would you feel like if there was to be a war, if there was to be universal carnage? Am I just talking some morbid rant? My friends, these are the facts of life, and failure to prepare for them is not only foolhardiness, it is a display of lack of intelligence. It is to put ourselves in the position of men and women who trust to luck and have no philosophy of life. The spies have entered. Mighty things may be in the offing. In any case we all have to meet God. Are we prepared, or have we been living the careless life?

If we do not heed the warning the last characteristic of this life to which I want to refer will be true of us as it was true of these people—suicidal. This life is selfish, small, short-sighted, but above all it is suicidal. "And there was no deliverer." These wretched people were responsible for their own disaster because they had cut off their own communications, and then the six hundred men came and they were too far away from Zidon, and they had not traded with anyone; they had lived a circumscribed life.

The godless life may be highly successful for a while. Men have lived it and boasted of its wonders and joys. But what happens in the time of crisis? Have you a deliverer, a friend? Do you know of someone to whom you can turn in the moment of your greatest trial? Are your lines of communication open? Have you preserved a way of retreat? The Zidonians had cut themselves off, and that led to their fate.

But, thank God, I have something further to tell you. There is a New Testament in addition to the Old. We have all been like the Zidonians. All of us by nature have cut ourselves off from God. But then the crisis comes and we turn to find God. We feel we are cads because we have ignored him for years and only turn to him when we need him. But thanks be unto God, into this iniquitous colony that mankind has made of the world, God sent his only begotten Son. He made a way out, a way of deliverance, a way of release, a way of salvation. Christ came to bring us to God, and, knowing him, whatever the need, whatever the crisis, God is always at hand and we are not forsaken. The spies have come, but, thank God, the Son of God, the Savior of man, has come also.

> There is a way for man to rise
> To that sublime abode
> An offering and a sacrifice
> A Holy Spirit's energies,
> An Advocate with God.

While there is yet time, get to know the Savior. Start on the road that leads to the everlasting city.

6

The Motive and Methods
of the Missionary Enterprise

*. . . I am made all things to all men, that I might by
all means save some.* (1 Cor. 9:22)

There is surely nothing in the life of the church
at large, or in the life of the individual Christian, that raises
so many fundamental problems and questions as the matter
of the missionary enterprise of the church. I would not
hesitate to state that finally there is no more thorough test of
our individual profession of faith than our attitude toward
this question.

The history of the church in the past abundantly justifies
us in making that statement. From the very earliest days, as
recorded in the Book of the Acts of the Apostles, right down
to our own time, every true revival of religion, every
reawakening of the spiritual life and consciousness of the
church has invariably led to missionary activity. It seems to
have followed as the night the day that when men have
experienced and enjoyed the blessings of the gospel themselves, they have felt a burning desire and passion to share

Preached in the City Temple on behalf of the Colonial Missionary Society this blessed experience with others. That, therefore, being the rule, we cannot escape the inevitable corollary that it becomes also a test of our condition. Are we aware of the same desire? Do we react in the same way?

But apart from this test, the missionary enterprise—when we face it, or when we are asked to face it in a meeting or in a book—of necessity causes us to consider ultimate questions. We may have been nurtured in a Christian atmosphere, we may have accepted the gospel and its teaching, and all our lives we may have done our utmost to live by its standard. But still our attitude may have been mainly negative; and, indeed, to a very large extent, even thoughtless. This kind of life, we decided, was the best for us—we enjoy it and are glad that we are in it; the danger is that we may just continue to enjoy it in this way without thinking more deeply about it.

Nothing is so likely to awaken us out of such a condition, and force us to return to a consideration of the elemental truths of the Christian faith, as the missionary enterprise. The reason is that it raises questions that demand an answer: Why send men and women abroad to other countries to preach the gospel? Why create elaborate organizations and make such efforts to maintain them? Why interfere in the lives and customs of people of other races? Why upset the beliefs and traditions that have apparently satisfied these people through many long centuries? What is our sanction for so doing? What is there in our faith and in our belief that not only entitles us to do so, but indeed compels us to do so? Such are the questions that must arise; and the answers to them will involve the whole basis of our Christian profession.

As I need scarcely remind you, what I have thus stated is exactly what is happening in the church at the present time. For various reasons, many of them of a purely practical nature, the missionary question, as we have come to call it, has been occupying much of the attention of the church for many years. The matter has been considered from all possible angles, but I think it will be agreed that the problem finally resolves itself into the discussion of two matters—the message and the method.

As we come to consider these questions, there is surely nothing better that we can do than to ponder once more what the greatest authority on the subject had to say. Paul still stands out as the greatest missionary of all time, judged by any standard—zeal, experience, or results. And here, in his first Epistle to the Corinthians, he is particularly enlightening and instructive on this question. What he has to say about the message is, of course, to be found in every Epistle he ever wrote. What makes this one of special interest is that in it he also deals with the question of method. He does so to defend himself. Certain people in Corinth had been criticizing him in a very drastic manner. They had actually questioned his right to call himself an apostle at all. They had raised queries as to his knowledge, and many had come to the conclusion that because he had not taught them anything beyond "Jesus Christ and him crucified" he really knew nothing beyond that. Others criticized his method and manner of speech—the absence of the usual rhetorical and oratorical methods and devices. And even Paul's refusal to accept any payment from them had come to be regarded by many as being nothing but an indication of subtlety and duplicity of character. In other words, his whole conduct among them as a missionary proclaiming the gospel had been questioned.

While it cannot be said that Paul's object in writing this letter was merely to defend himself—his main motive was to restore order in the church, and to save her from the terrible dangers that threatened her—at the same time his refutation of the charges against him run as a kind of leitmotif throughout the Epistle. Here in this ninth chapter, and especially in the last section, we have what we can surely call the most definite and explicit statement that the apostle ever made on the question of both the missionary message and method. One phrase epitomizes it perfectly: "I am

made all things to all men, that I might by all means save
some'' (v. 22). I will consider this statement and its context
along the following lines.

The Purpose

We must start with what we may call the object or the
purpose of missionary endeavor and effort. I say we must
"start" with this, not, however, because I subscribe to the
philosophy that the end justifies the means, but because it
should be obvious that in this matter the end, of necessity,
controls and determines the means and insists on their being
in accordance with it. Within the space of four verses Paul
mentions the object and the purpose of all his missionary
striving six times. Five times he expresses it as a desire to
"save" men. That is the goal for which he sets out, and it is
because of that that he is prepared to do the various things
he mentions. Never for a moment did he lose sight of the
objective.

I take it that one of the functions of the preacher of this
colonial missionary sermon is to call attention to this, and to
help the society and all its members, and indeed the entire
church, to examine itself and its true motive. There is a
sense in which it can be said that the whole message of the
Bible, from beginning to end, is just an appeal to men to
keep their eyes fixed on the ultimate goal of life, and a
warning to beware lest they settle down and become content
with anything else than the ultimate vision of God. In our
personal lives we always need that exhortation, and it is
equally the need of the church at large in her various
activities. There is always the danger of falling back on
secondary and lesser loyalties and motives, and of trying to
rationalize that procedure. It is not that we are deliberately
dishonest, but that all our natures are "desperately wicked
and deceitful," and that "we wrestle not against flesh and
blood, but against principalities, against powers, against the
rulers of the darkness of this world, against spiritual wick-

edness in high places'' (Eph. 6:12). Or, if you prefer it, it is essential that we shall examine ourselves and our motives from time to time because there is far too much truth in what modern psychology has to say about human nature! Let us then glance at some of the lesser and, at times, false motives that are forever trying to infiltrate our missionary activity.

Secondary Motives

There is ever the danger which arises from the machine itself. This is something that is being recognized more and more in the secular world. Machinery, which should be the servant of man, has rapidly become man's master. We hear much today of the tyranny of the machine. Precisely the same thing is true of the mechanism or the machinery of church work. At the beginning there is a great vision granted to an individual or a group, and, consumed with a burning passion, they set out to accomplish the work. In order to do so they have to establish a certain organization, a certain machinery. That is as it should be. But after a while the vision fades, the zeal and the passion wane. The machinery, however, is still in existence and has to be maintained, the work is still there and has to be carried on; and we tend to carry on simply for the sake of carrying on. I have often heard appeals for contributions to missionary funds made solely in terms of avoiding the failure of the machinery. Indeed, at times the appeal has been even lower. Churches have been asked simply to maintain their own standard of giving, thus to maintain their own status!

How easy also to confuse the political and the spiritual motives in this matter; and especially when we are thinking of the British Empire. This may not be so great a danger today as it was in the last century, but occasionally one hears echoes of it still, and observes the tendency to regard missionary and imperialistic motives as being identical. It is perhaps natural and legitimate that we should feel a special concern for those who are nearest and dearest. But according to the New Testament my desire should not be that my family or my nation shall be Christian because it happens to be mine, but rather that I should desire it to be Christian. A distinction between Colonial and general is legitimate only as regards organization. It is utterly intolerable and un-Christian if it intrudes into the realm of the spiritual objective at which we aim.

Another motive that is ever ready to offer itself is that of a general desire to help others and to better their condition: a general expression of our humanitarian instincts, or a more specific expression of our particular political philosophy. Here we stand on very dangerous ground, and we must carefully avoid being misunderstood. We all surely do and must believe in educational and medical work, as we must also believe in an equality of opportunity for all men. But are we ever to allow such activities to become the primary work of the church and the final goal of her ambition? As a general expression of the Christian character they are beyond praise; as an aid to the primary work of the church, a work which she alone can perform, they are more than invaluable. But should we ever rest content with them, and allow them to monopolize our attention and our energy, they will become the very instruments of Satan in our hands.

But what is the real objective? What is the true goal? Paul's answer is unequivocal, as has been the answer of the great missionaries of all centuries. It is to "gain" men (KJV), to "save" men. Paul traveled day and night across continents and seas, and labored without ceasing, for that reason and that reason only. Men had become lost, they had become the slaves of darkness and of sin, they were alienated from God, rebels against him and his law, and therefore under condemnation and under wrath. Their position was desperate, though they did not realize it. They must be roused, they must be warned, they must be brought to repentance; and what is still more important, they must be shown the one and only way of escape, which was to be found in Jesus Christ and him crucified. Here was a message from God himself, offering pardon and forgiveness and a new life in Christ. Men must be saved from the dominion of Satan and translated into the kingdom of the Son of God. An entirely new way of life was possible for them in this world, and in the world to come were laid up for them things which "Eye hath not seen nor ear heard, neither have entered into the heart of man . . ." (1 Cor. 2:9). To gain men from the life of this present world for this other new life, to save them from all the possible consequences of their sin by means of the gospel of Christ, was the apostle's one ambition. And it must ever remain the central message of the gospel and the primary goal and objective of all missionary endeavor.

Our Attitude Toward Other Faiths

That being the objective, we find ourselves at once face to face with another question: namely, how it is to be reached. Or, to change our terms, we must consider the question of methods—our missionary plan.

Here again we deal with a very controversial matter, one that is occupying a great deal of attention at the present time. Paul's phrase crystallizes the whole question perfectly. He says that he is "made all things to all men" that he might "thereby save some." What exactly does that mean? And what do those other phrases mean—"and unto the Jews I became a Jew, that I might gain the Jews" and "to them that are under the law as under the law" and "to them that are without law as without law"? Our answer to that question will depend ultimately on our view of the truth—as to whether we regard it as relative or absolute.

Some would say that the one thing that matters, the one thing which is of vital importance in the matter of method, is that we should study the people among whom we propose to work. We must get to understand their psychology, we must study their faith, their mode of life, and the views that they have always held. Having done so, we must approach them, not to tell them that they have been altogether in the dark and entirely mistaken, but rather to tell them that we value very highly the aspects of the truth that are emphasized in their religion, and that we now suggest that they should likewise consider other aspects of the truth that are emphasized in *our* religion. I desire to be scrupulously fair to this point of view—so I would add that those who hold it often go further and say that we should indicate that ours is superior, and that, of all the religious geniuses the world has ever seen, Jesus of Nazareth was the greatest. Being "all things to all men" means, according to this view, deliberately looking for and praising the good elements in all the religions of the world, to arrive at the ultimate synthesis.

Paul's Answer

Whatever one may think of this view, one thing is abundantly clear—it was not the view of Paul, and it certainly is the very antithesis of what he suggests here, as can be demonstrated by his qualifying statements. (Curiously enough, one of them is not to be found in the Authorized Version, but is in all modern translations, the Revised Version included.) Paul writes, "To them that are under the law, as under the law"—but he immediately adds, "not being myself under the law." Then again, "to them that are without law as without law"—but again in brackets, "being not without law to God, but under the law to Christ." (See vv. 20–21.)

Why is Paul so quick to add these qualifying and limiting statements? It is his purpose to show that he can brook no false tolerance or false accommodation with respect to the truth itself. Being "as under the law" does not mean that he is actually under it; being "as without law" must not be construed to mean that he is lawless or Antinomian.

Indeed, there is a sense in which at first the apostle seems to be contradicting himself in this Epistle. He says that he "is made all things to all men that he might thereby save some."

To the Jew he appeals in one way and to the Gentile in another; and yet, knowing that the Greeks love philosophy and wisdom and rhetoric and eloquence, he says that he *determined* not to know anything among them "save Jesus Christ and Him crucified." He knew the psychology of the Greek; he was aware of the fact that the preaching of the cross would of necessity be foolishness to the Greek mind; yet he not only preached that, but deliberately confined his message to it. How can that be reconciled with being "all things to all men"?

It is a question of placing the truth, and the desire for the success of the missionary enterprise, in their correct positions. For me to be quite fair, let me add that often those who have been most orthodox have erred quite as much as those who hold the view we have already considered. They have erred by pressing the matter to the opposite extreme, saying that nothing matters but the knowledge of the truth, and that a knowledge of the psychology and background of the people is quite unnecessary. (This tendency to exalt method at the expense of truth, or truth at the expense of method, is not confined to the missionary problem. There is a type of medical doctor who is more concerned with studying the patient than the disease; but there is the other type who is so absorbed by his interest in the disease that he forgets the patient. The first may have a wonderful bedside manner, and his visits may always make the patient feel better and happier; but if he lacks the capacity and knowledge to diagnose and to cure the disease, from the standpoint of scientific medicine he is not only a complete failure but also a positive danger. The second doctor may have great theoretical knowledge and may know all there is to be known about disease processes; but if he lacks a clinical sense and the ability to understand his patient and apply his knowledge to that individual case, he will be equally useless.)

Paul avoids both extremes. On the question of the truth he is adamant—"For other foundation can no man lay than that is laid, which is Jesus Christ" (3:11). Christ is the only Savior or else not a Savior at all. "There is none other name under heaven given among men, whereby we must be saved" (Acts 4:12). There is no second name, there can be none—he is unique, he is the Father's last word, he is the only begotten Son. Nothing and no one can add anything to what he has done, and any attempt to add anything to his gospel, though it be the very law that God gave the Jews, is to subtract everything from it. The truth as it is in Jesus is absolute, the central message of salvation in Christ is final. No accommodation, therefore, concerning that!

But having said that, accommodate to the very hilt. In matters indifferent, in matters that are not vital to a man's whole standing before God, as much elasticity and accommodation as possible. The Christian is not merely to state the truth; he is to state it in such a way as to "gain" men, to win them to the truth. He is not to tamper with the message of which he is but a steward; but at the same time he is to be the very opposite of the type of man who is so concerned about his own orthodoxy, and so proud of it, that he becomes a stumbling block to his weaker brother, and altogether forgets the lost souls about him.

O that the church had always followed the great apostle's example! God grant that we may be given grace to follow it, and grace also to trust ultimately for success to the power of God, instead of to our own wisdom and knowledge.

The Missionary Passion

I have time for but a word on the last matter. But it must be said, because it breathes through all the apostle's words in this Epistle as well as throughout his letters and in his verbal discourses. I refer to what we may call the missionary zeal or the missionary passion: "I am made all things to all men that I might by all means save some." "Necessity is laid on me." "Woe is unto me if I preach not the gospel."

What was the source of this passion? What gave birth to it? He tells us, "And this I do for the gospel's sake, that I might be partaker thereof with you" (1 Cor. 9:23). The gospel of Christ had already meant everything to Paul. It had given him everything that was of any value, and had made all else worthless and valueless. But there was more to come, and he desired to be partaker of that also.

The gospel must be preached to all, were it merely that Christ had commanded that it should be preached to all nations everywhere; a mere sense of duty and of loyalty to the Lord should urge us to do so. But there is something more. He died that we might be delivered, but he is "the propitiation not only for our sins, but also for the sins of the whole world." Can we refrain from telling those who are ignorant of that, and who, if they knew it and believed it, might be partakers in our joy and in our blessed hope?

That is the source of the passion. But how does it express itself? Paul was "free from all men," yet he "made himself servant unto all that he might gain some." He waived his own right and submitted himself to all kinds of indignities, trials, and persecutions; more than that, he tells us that he waged a constant warfare with his own sinful nature. His personal life and mode of living were as rigorous as those of the athlete striving for the prize. He buffeted and bruised his body to bring it into subjection, that he might do his work perfectly and please his Master.

That is how his passion expressed itself. He gave himself, he gave all—not an occasional grudging contribution, not an unwilling attendance at an occasional meeting, and a prayer now and again for the success of the work when he chanced to think of it, but a life with all its amazing gifts and powers entirely devoted to the cause.

Is there any reason why Paul should be thus devoted, more than any other Christian? We cannot claim his gifts, and we have not received his special call to be an apostle, nor have we seen the risen Lord as he saw him that day on the way to Damascus; but the same Lord has died for us, our debt to him is equally great. We cannot all go abroad to preach about him to the teeming masses, but are we doing what is easily within our reach by way of prayer and material support? Are we prepared to deny ourselves and to forego things which are perfectly legitimate and lawful to us, for his sake and for the sake of those who know him not?

I leave the question with you and with myself. God grant that our response to it may be a willing and entire surrender of ourselves to Christ and to his service.

7

The Science of Sin

And it came to pass, as Peter passed throughout all quarters, he came down also to the saints which dwelt at Lydda. And there he found a certain man named Aeneas, which had kept his bed eight years, and was sick of the palsy. And Peter said unto him, Aeneas, Jesus Christ maketh thee whole: arise, and make thy bed. And he arose immediately. And all that dwelt at Lydda and Saron saw him, and turned to the Lord. (Acts 9:32–35)

It has been the custom among certain people who claim for themselves an unusual degree of learning and culture, to cast a good deal of doubt on the historical value of the early chapters of the Book of the Acts of the Apostles. These people tell us they are quite prepared to accept the Gospels of Matthew, Mark, and Luke as being more or less an accurate account of the life of Jesus, but that they cannot accept the early chapters of Acts, nor the Gospel according to John, nor the claims made in the various Epistles, especially by Paul. In other words they are prepared to accept the simple gospel, but they cannot accept the addi-

Preached in Westminster Chapel

tional claims that are made in the various other books in the New Testament.

These people display in their position a good deal of consistency, for it would be rather surprising were they to accept these early chapters of Acts as being historical, after having denied the unique deity of Christ and the fact of his miracles. This Book of Acts not only claims that Christ possessed divine and miraculous power; it also makes the astonishing claim that the ordinary, simple, and more or less ignorant men and women who had banded together in his name, had become possessed of that same supernatural and miraculous power. So, unwittingly, these critics are making the rather important statement that the Book of Acts is the finest commentary that we possess on the exalted claims made for Jesus in the four Gospels. Indeed, I would go a step further and say that there is a sense in which you cannot understand the Gospels at all except you read them in the light of this Book of Acts of the Apostles.

The Witness of the Acts

I am convinced that half the trouble that people are finding with religion these days is because they are spending far too much time reading the Gospels, and far too little time reading the Acts of the Apostles and the subsequent history of the Christian church. People have read the sayings and doings of Jesus and are unable to understand them, as was inevitable; they have failed to consider the evidence before them. In other words, if instead of trying to unravel the eternal mystery of the gospel, men and women would simply study a little more church history, they would soon discover the explanation of much that is at present inexplicable to them.

What I am suggesting is that they approach the great doctrines of Christianity directly instead of indirectly. Take, for example, the doctrine of the incarnation, that great mystery that tells us that the eternal substance was made

flesh and dwelt among us. Who can understand such a
mystery? The human mind is baffled by the very idea of it.
My position is not that I claim to understand the incarnation; it is that I am aware of certain facts in my experience—
and in the experience of others who have belonged to the
Christian church—that simply force me to believe in the
incarnation because it is the only explanation that is
adequate.

The same is true of the doctrine of the atonement. No
mind is big enough to understand the mystery of that great
doctrine; it is too vast. I do not claim that I understand the
atonement, but there are great facts in the history of the
Christian church that I cannot understand at all except in
the light of the atonement.

It is the same with the doctrine of the resurrection, which
tells us that on the morning of the third day Christ forced
asunder the bands of death, and rose triumphant from the
tomb. No mind can measure such a mighty fact. I do not
understand the resurrection, but when I look into the faces
of certain men who once were drunkards and gamblers,
blasphemers and wife beaters, and who are now saints of
God, I am simply bound to believe in the resurrection, for
there is no other power under heaven great enough to
account for such an amazing transformation of human life.

What I am suggesting is that we should approach these
doctrines of our faith in the light of the history of the
Christian church. The Book of Acts is essentially a commentary on the statements contained in the four Gospels. There
are, indeed, certain things in the Gospels that are quite
meaningless if you do not accept the early chapters of Acts.
We know that Jesus told his disciples, "It is expedient for
you that I go away; if I go not away the Comforter will not
come unto you." And on another occasion our Lord turned
to his disciples and said, "Greater works than these shall ye
do because I go unto the Father." That is a meaningless
statement unless we accept the record of this Book of Acts,
where we find that the preaching of Peter and Paul was

actually a greater success than the preaching of Christ himself. Yes, this Book of Acts is indeed a commentary on the Gospels.

In every chapter and in almost every verse, this book reminds us that the central business of the Christian church is not merely to perpetuate the memory of Christ, but rather to manifest and to mediate the power of Christ. According to the Acts of the Apostles, its task is not merely to tell people what Jesus said and did. No, the church is the body of Christ, and its task is to mediate his power in the world. It is his body, through which he works and acts. In other words, this book claims that the church is supernatural, and is itself a divine institution.

Now that is a very important principle, and one that we need to remember as we read the Acts of the Apostles. The claim the Gospels make for Jesus is not simply that he was better than anyone else; their claim is that he was altogether different and unique. He ascended to greater heights than anyone who has ever lived. He is, in fact, the Son of God from heaven. And with regard to the sayings of Christ, there is a sense in which the Gospels put the emphasis not so much on what he said, as the way in which he said it. Have you ever stood in your imagination with the congregations who listened to the teaching of Jesus? What do those people say to one another? Do they say, "What a remarkably learned discourse that was! How vast his knowledge! How deep is his acquaintance with scientific thought"? No, that is not their comment. Their comment is, rather, "This man speaketh with authority, and not as the scribes." They say, "Never man spake like this Man." It was not so much what he said as the way in which he said it. They felt his uniqueness; they felt the supernatural element in his nature.

The Uniqueness of the Christ

Precisely the same claim is made for the Christian church in the Acts of the Apostles. It is important that we should

understand what the real function of the church is. Men are
looking to her for so many different things; but the main
function of the church is to be the body of Christ, to be the
vehicle through which he does his own miraculous and
mighty work. The church is not comparable to any other
institution; she is unique, separate. And of all the miracles
that she works, the greatest is still that ancient miracle that
she has worked throughout the centuries: the miracle of
turning sinners into saints.

As to how she works that miracle, I would remind you of
an incident in which a miracle worked by Peter provides a
parable of the whole function of the Christian church
(9:32–35). Peter was making a his rounds of a number of the
churches and "he came down also to the saints which dwelt
at Lydda" (v. 32). All that we are told about his visit there
was that "he found a certain man named Aeneas, which had
kept his bed eight years, and was sick of the palsy [paraly-
sis]." Peter found this man in bed unable to move. There he
was laying on his back. I can tell you a number of things
about this man, Aeneas. One thing I can tell you is this: he
wasn't lying there because he was lazy or because he didn't
want to walk or work. That wasn't his trouble; he couldn't
move from his bed because of his infirmity. Another thing I
can tell you about him is this: his mind and his brain were
perfectly normal. You could have engaged him in conversa-
tion concerning things that usually occupy the minds of men
and women. I would go further and say that you could have
discussed with him the whole question of walking, and he
could have expressed his opinion as to how men walked. He
desired to walk; he made efforts that he might walk; but his
trouble was that somewhere between his normal brain and
his muscles and limbs there was powerlessness—some blem-
ish in his nervous system the result of which was that those
perfectly good impulses originating in his brain were never
allowed to pass through into his limbs. This man was not
whole; he was divided into two, one half normal, and the
other half abnormal. The result was a lack of coordination—

one half of him trying to move, and the other half making it impossible for him to move.

I wonder whether I need point out that what I have been saying about this man's body is true also of the soul and the spirit of man. Is lack of coordination not an appropriate description of that condition we call sin? Is it not accurate to say that the tragedy of mankind is that man knows what he ought to do, but cannot do it? Everyone knows the difference between good and evil. But man is conscious of something in his nature that keeps him from doing the good that he knows.

For example, you may be walking down the street one day, and you see on the other side someone with whom you've had a quarrel; you haven't spoken to each other for years. But on this particular day the impulse suddenly comes to you to pull yourself together and do the big thing for once, to cross the road, to hold out your hand to that individual, and say, "It was more my fault than yours; come, let us forgive and forget." Then in a flash there comes the thought, Why should I stoop? Why must I always be the one to give in? And the result is that you let that opportunity for reconciliation slip by. The impulse came, but it was never translated into action. Is that not a common experience for all of us? There are times in each of our lives when we feel that we must do better, that we must be kind at home, that we must go to the help of those in need. The impulse comes, but we never act on it. This paralysis in the soul, this thing which prevents action, is the disease of mankind. The trouble with the world today is not that it does not know what it ought to be; it is that it somehow lacks the power which alone can enable it to do it. And the business of the church is to link men and women to the power that will enable them to do the right.

The Saving Christ

How does the church do that? The answer is found in this incident. The first thing I read in this passage is that Peter

came and found Aeneas (v. 33). Man has taken the Sermon
on the Mount as a kind of basis for his social gospel. But the
moment he tries to live it, he discovers his paralysis.

If you would like to know just how paralyzed Aeneas is,
try to find God in your own strength. You will realize that
Aeneas could not find Peter because he was suffering from
the palsy. But by the grace of God Peter found Aeneas, and
he spoke the words that set him free and enabled him to
walk. Now that is exactly what the church has always done.
Her history has been a story of ups and downs. Certain
rationalists from this country were so certain that Christianity was finished that they said it wasn't even worth their
opposition. But just as they were uttering their funeral
oration over the dead body of the church, God sent his Peter
in the person of John Wesley, and through what was nearly
a moribund institution there went revival power and
reawakening.

And so it has been throughout the history of the church.
You need not worry about the future of the Christian
church. God will send his Peter. And what has been true of
the church in general has been equally true of individual
Christians through the ages: after much searching they at
last see the gleam. "And Peter said unto him, Aeneas, Jesus
Christ maketh thee whole: arise, and make thy bed." It
always happens that way.

I must include a word about the time element in this
particular miracle. According to the story, this man rose
immediately. It wasn't a process. He didn't read a lot of
books or attend various meetings. I remember the ancient
discussion that used to occupy our time and attention in
Sunday school and Bible class—the question whether conversion was sudden or gradual; there were always the two
sides. But I would point out that the wrong question was
being discussed. The question was not so much whether
conversion was sudden or gradual, but rather, Have you
been converted? Is your life whole? Have you come into
contact with the power of God? Peter made the simple

announcement to Aeneas, "Jesus Christ maketh thee whole." The whole business of the church is to proclaim to bewildered men and women that Jesus of Nazareth is the Son of God who came into this world to bear our sins, to make us whole, and to set us free.

8

The Divine Wisdom

If any of you lack wisdom, let him ask of God, that giveth to all men liberally, and upbraideth not; and it shall be given him. But let him ask in faith, nothing wavering. For he that wavereth is like a wave of the sea driven with the wind and tossed. For let not that man think that he shall receive any thing of the Lord. A double minded man is unstable in all his ways. (James 1:5–8)

The words of James 1:5–8 are a direct sequel to the remarkable exhortation that we are to "count it all joy when [we] fall into divers temptations" (v. 2). We are, James is telling us, to look positively at difficulties and trials so as to work them out in such a way that we end by praising God for them, thus finding our joy increased. The natural man of course will be tempted to say, "It is a wonderful exhortation, but it asks a man to do that which human nature is not capable of doing. It might be all right for those exceptional people who give themselves exclusively to the nurture of the Christian life, or for the hermit who spends his time in prayer and meditation, or for the man who

Preached in Westminster Chapel

scorns everything that the world has to offer; but this counsel is quite beyond the realization of the average person."

Let me remind the person who reasons in such a way that these words were written by none other than James, a very practical man. Surely that fact ought to help us face up to this exhortation instead of running away from it. One's natural instinct might tempt him to say, "This is not for me." But in so thinking, one will miss one of the most amazing blessings that God offers to the Christian.

But James will not allow us to rob ourselves of this blessing which God is waiting and willing to give us, so he proceeds to deal with the imaginary objections. He says, "If any of you feel that this is something that is entirely beyond you, then let me show you how you may actually attain it." We ought to be grateful to this practical man, who, not content merely to state his case, proceeds to apply it, and helps us to apply it to our own lives.

The Quest for Wisdom

The word *wisdom* is found frequently in the Bible. It is a word that has oftentimes engaged the attention of learned men. To the Greeks, wisdom connoted understanding, learning, and insight into mysteries. There was among them a desire for knowledge and a craving for understanding; they were intent on their quest for wisdom. These men of intellect spent their time listening to great teachers and rhetoricians discuss the meaning of life, propounding various theories in their search for enlightenment and understanding. The word *wisdom* appears frequently in the literature of the Old Testament. In fact, certain parts of the Old Testament are given the title "Wisdom Literature." However, the wisdom referred to in the Old Testament is very different from the wisdom as understood by the Greeks. Wisdom in the Bible means not so much understanding and intellectual ability, as the correct use of those

things. It refers not so much to man's intellectual capacity
for grasping philosophical theories, as to the whole orientation of his life, the whole point of his existence. When James
used the word, he was using it in the Hebrew sense rather
than in the Greek sense. His statement, therefore, means,
"If any of you lack this fundamental attitude, this central
outlook, let him ask of God . . . and it shall be given him."

Two Ways of Wisdom

Now to be practical—and we are living in days when we
need, more than at any other time, to be simple and
practical—let us consider in what respects we have need of
this wisdom. James was writing to those who were passing
through trying times, and facing serious difficulties; and he
exhorts them to count it all joy that they are found in such
a state. He says that if they need wisdom to do that he will
show them how they may obtain it. First and foremost, they
needed a wisdom that would enable them to look at life, and
its attendant circumstances, so as to be able to rejoice in
them.

Paul very often dwells on this particular theme. In his
First Epistle to the Corinthians he shows how entirely
different is the wisdom of the Christians from that of the
Greeks. He says, "For after that in the wisdom of God the
world by wisdom knew not God, it pleased God by the
foolishness of preaching to save them that believe" (1:21).
However much knowledge a man might have, it does not
enable him to count it a joy when he falls into divers
temptations and trials. In order to substantiate that statement we have only to look around us, or to read the
biographies and study history. However great a man may be
in a natural sense, he will fail to rise to this particular height.
He must see life from an entirely new angle; he must possess
a new view of it; he must attain to a spiritual understanding.
If a man lives only for this world and for the things it has to

offer, if he lives only for ease and pleasure and comfort, if this world means everything to him, then it is perfectly obvious, in a time like the present, he cannot really be happy since everything he likes is being taken from him, and everything that he dislikes is happening all around him. There is only one way in which a man can rejoice—by viewing life from a spiritual angle, and knowing something of those things which the eye of man has not seen, nor his ear heard, and which God has prepared for those who love him. He needs, in fact, to be so directly related to God that he knows for certain that whatever men may do they can never rob him of his supreme possession, which is his relationship to God through Jesus Christ. We need wisdom and understanding to work out what is happening to us. Similarly, we need wisdom so to order our lives that we shall derive the maximum amount of benefit from the things that are happening to us. We need this new orientation so that these things may lead us still nearer to God.

More practical still is the need for wisdom to enable us to reach right decisions in any given circumstance. How difficult it is sometimes to know exactly what to do; how difficult it is sometimes to know how to act, and how to react. I may be confronted with a number of possibilities; I need wisdom that I may do that which is right, and that which is best. What am I to do? When I come to the crossroads, which way am I to take? Here again earthly wisdom proves itself utterly useless. Our supreme need is for some higher guidance—guidance from God himself. We stand in need of wisdom, says James; we need spiritual enlightenment to know how to do the best things in life.

In this world we are apt to think that only some exceptional people are capable of wisdom, that the wise man is the man of learning and of knowledge and of intellectual understanding; whereas the average man, and the one who is below average, know nothing of real wisdom. But our text reminds us of one of the central glories of the gospel of Jesus Christ—that this gift of wisdom is not the possession merely of a chosen few, but is something available to all. James says, "If *any* of you," and "God giveth to *all* men liberally (italics added)." Here is the most remarkable thing of all. While the world and its philosophers fail to attain these things, yet, wonder of wonders, it has been the possession of humble, lowly, and insignificant people. You have only to read the story of the Christian church to realize that what James here offered to these people was something tangible, something that has been an actuality in the lives of countless thousands of people. God chose the foolish things of the world to confound the mighty; the worldly man, in spite of all his efforts, never succeeds in attaining to such heights. You read the story of ordinary, simple men, and you find that they actually did rejoice in tribulation. You read of those slaves, who, in the early centuries, literally praised God when they suffered for his name's sake. You read of those who were despoiled of everything and cast into prison, and yet they were able to glory in the Lord. The truth of these words of James is exemplified in the lives of thousands of ordinary people who knew God in such a way that everything that happened to them simply served to draw them nearer to him. And James says that anyone—regardless of position—feeling the need of this wisdom, may receive it.

Someone may be tempted to respond, "What you say is perfectly right, but it doesn't apply to me. I have turned my back on God; I have neglected him." To such a one James says, "You need not be afraid that if you turn to God now he will not be interested in you; God does not recriminate. If you feel your need of wisdom ask God for it, and he will give it you freely, without recrimination."

If you are at your wits' end, then turn to God just as you are and he will give you the wisdom that you need. He will not upbraid you; he will not cast your sins into your face. No, he will receive you. There is no limit to his offer. It is not our ability that matters; it is not even our righteousness.

Though we are weak, and ignorant, and sinful, if we but turn to him, he will give us his blessing.

Only One Condition

There is only one condition. "Let him ask in faith, nothing wavering." James compares the uncertain man to the waves of the sea, tossing hither and thither, without control. "A double-minded man," he writes, "is unstable in all his ways."

The one condition is that we should have faith in God—we must really desire to be on God's side. The trouble with so many people is that they want to make the best of two worlds. They don't know exactly which side they're on. They want to be Christians, but at the same time they want to be worldlings. They desire to be on both sides. And the result is that when they turn to God during a crisis, they feel they really have no right to pray; they are uncertain of themselves, and so tend also to be uncertain of God. James says, "For he that wavereth is like a wave of the sea driven with the wind and tossed. . . . let not that man think that he shall receive anything of the Lord" (vv. 6–7). The one condition is that I should be wholeheartedly on God's side. He asks for a wholehearted consecration. Everything else must go that I may be right with him.

Are we really on God's side? Are we prepared to surrender ourselves to God, to forsake the world and all its ways? Are we determined to put an end to this condition of divided allegiance, and to declare ourselves wholeheartedly on the side of God? If so, and if in our turn we ask God for his divine wisdom, we shall certainly receive it. We shall have that spiritual understanding that will enable us to count all things as ministering to our joy in Christ Jesus our Lord. God grant that, yielding ourselves entirely unto him, we may fulfil that one condition, and receive this wisdom divine.

9

A Little Maid's Testimony

*And the Syrians . . . had brought away captive out
of the land of Israel a little maid; and she waited on
Naaman's wife. And she said unto her mistress,
Would God my lord were with the prophet that is in
Samaria! for he would recover him of his leprosy.
And one went in, and told his lord, saying, Thus
and thus said the maid that is of the land of Israel.*
(2 Kings 5:2–4)

There is a grave danger on the part of Christian
people today of forgetting that we are to present to the
world a specific message. The tendency is to apply the gospel
of Christ to the present situation in a general sense. We talk
about the forces that are in conflict in the world, we
consider the present state of the nations, and we try to apply
the message of the gospel to that general situation. But the
function of the gospel is something that is intensely personal.
Many sermons and addresses delivered today seem to lack a
unique Christian note—they might just as well be given by
those who do not claim to be Christians at all. If our message
is the kind that might just as well be given by those

Preached in Westminster Chapel

concerned solely about secular affairs, that message is not specifically Christian. As we read the New Testament we find that the message given by the early Christians was altogether different from anything that the world knew. It was a unique message, one which no one could give save he who was truly Christian. The task of the Christian is something entirely separate and distinct from anything the world—even at its very best and highest—is capable of.

Christians fail to realize the remarkable opportunity presenting itself today. Both the history of the Bible and that of the church illustrate the fact that there are times and periods when special opportunities present themselves to the church and to individual Christians. Surely this present time is one of those occasions. Men and women outside the church are looking to Christianity, wondering whether, after all, the solution for the world's problems is not to be found in the gospel of Christ; therein lies your opportunity and mine. Are we grasping these opportunities, seeking to bring these men and women into touch with the one who alone can satisfy the desires of the human soul?

The Wisdom of the Simple

It is against this background that I want to call attention to the familiar Old Testament story of Naaman. However, I desire to call special attention not to him, but to the little maid—whose name we do not even know—who worked in his household. Here we have a simple illustration of the way in which God uses the weak things of the world to confound the mighty and strong. We see also in this story that Christianity is something that is invincible. It doesn't matter where you put the Christian; if he is truly Christ's he is bound to triumph. Even in adversity he finds himself capable of doing something that will ultimately make him triumphant. The Christian possesses a knowledge that is greater than the knowledge of the greatest outside Christ. The humblest Christian is superior to the greatest worldling.

Here is the story of a little maid who, though she performed the most menial of tasks, knew something of which a great captain of the hosts of Syria was utterly ignorant.

There is nothing so interesting, as you read through the Bible, as seeing the way in which quite insignificant people seem to emerge in a crisis as the possessors of knowledge and understanding. When our Lord chose his disciples, he didn't go to the court of the king; he chose ordinary fishermen and workmen. And it was ever a matter of astonishment to the Sanhedrin, and to other courts, how these unlettered and ignorant men were able to perform mighty miracles.

Now Naaman's life was essentially a failure in spite of his greatness and might; he was really unhappy. Leprosy had come into his life and had spoiled everything. It mattered not how great his present glories were, or how many honors he might win in the future. Because he was a leper everything was nullified. All that the world could give him availed him nothing. That, of course, is a perfect parable of life in all times, and of life at this present hour. There is this canker, this disease, we call sin, which comes into life spoiling and—ultimately—ruining it. A man may possess every power that is available to mankind, but if he cannot solve that central problem of his life, he remains wretched and unhappy. But the wonder of the Christian is that the knowledge he possesses is a knowledge with regard to this leprosy called sin, and which meets just that vital and central need. In other words, the function of Christianity is to deal with and to solve this central problem of life; and the church is neglecting her true function unless she comes to the realization that that is her role.

The ultimate cause of the wretchedness and misery found in the human heart is not due to those things that follow in the wake of modern warfare; the ultimate cause is sin. The whole glory of the position of those who are Christians is this, that though we may not be able to solve great inter-

national problems, we do know the solution of the problem
of sin, as this little maid knew the secret of the cure of
Naaman's leprosy.

Knowledge and Testimony

Moreover, this marvelous knowledge is something which
even the humblest and the lowliest Christian can impart to
others. The little maid knew nothing about the nature of
leprosy; but she did know that there was a prophet who
"would recover him," and she just passed on that information concerning Elisha.

There is a tendency among Christians to think that only a
certain few are called on to do the work of an evangelist. It
is true that there are vocations in the church, and gifts
corresponding to those vocations; but the humblest and
lowliest Christian is capable of pointing souls to that One
who alone can solve the problem of sin, and to deliver men
and women from its tyranny. Let me ask a personal question. Are we individually alive to our present opportunity?
Are we seeking to bring peace and joy into burdened hearts?
We listen to those around us as they express their pessi-
mism, and their sense of hopelessness about the state of
things in the world. Do we do anything about it?

This little maid was filled with a sense of compassion and
sorrow as she thought of her master's leprosy; it became a
burden on her heart, so much so that she felt she must pass
on her knowledge to her mistress. Do we know anything
about the burden of souls? Do we feel a sense of sorrow for
the masses in their darkness and hopelessness? Or, are we
content to go on enjoying our own religion, never saying a
word to them? We know that their lives are blighted with
sin, and that blight might be cured if only we spoke a word
in season to them.

This little maid possessed a measure of the divine compassion. She and her people had been carried away captive
by Naaman and his hosts, and she might very well have

allowed him to go on suffering. But in spite of having been wronged, she forgave everything. You and I must be animated by this same spirit.

How great was this little maid's confidence in the power of Elisha! But we are able to point to One who is infinitely greater than that prophet. We can point to the very Son of God who has all power, and who has died to save us from sin. There is no depth of sin that he cannot plumb. There is no case too hopeless for him to rescue and redeem. God grant that in these days of opportunity we may feel this compelling power within to tell men and women of the Son of God, who, if they will but turn to him, will deliver them from their sins and fears, and give them new life.

10

The Preaching of the Cross

. . . we preach Christ crucified. . . . (1 Cor. 1:23)

Recently a question was put to me regarding the central verity of the Christian faith. The questioner asked me, "Why do you believe that the cross is God's way of saving men?" It is important that we spend time meditating on this most important and vital matter—for whatever may happen to nations or to men we must all face God at the end. Over and above the fate of earthly kingdoms is this matter of our eternal destiny.

In a sense, Christian preaching should always be the preaching of the cross; but there are certain times when we are especially called to consider it, to review the evidence, and to remind ourselves why it is we believe certain things. There is always the danger of our drifting away from our anchor—of forgetting to relate the whole of our Christian life to its fount and origin. Obviously, in one sermon no one can deal adequately with such a vast theme as why the cross is God's way of saving men. Yet I think the New Testament

Preached in Westminster Chapel

itself justifies a bird's-eye view of the whole question, and of reminding ourselves of certain basic postulates.

"Why do you believe that the cross is God's way of saving men?" I rather like the word *why* in that question, for it obviously calls for reasons. There are some who seem to think that the moment you come to the cross you cease to reason. But such a notion is utterly false from the standpoint of New Testament teaching. Sometimes you hear someone say, when discussing a certain preacher, "His view of the Bible seems to be all wrong, but he is very sound on the cross." It is imagined that as long as a man talks a great deal about the cross, his views concerning it must of necessity be right. There are people who interpret the death of our Lord as being nothing but an example of passive resistance, and they see nothing in it beyond that. I suggest that there is a sense in which there is greater need for thought and reasoning when we approach the cross than with regard to any other doctrine whatsoever.

The Teaching of the Bible

There are various reasons why I believe that the cross is God's way of saving men. The first and the most obvious is that it is clearly the teaching of the Bible. It is a matter of revelation, and not, primarily, a matter of experience. The experience alone does not and cannot explain to us how it is that the cross saves men. Truth alone can give enlightenment and understanding, and truth is to be found only in God's Word. Apart from the Bible, no one could ever say that the cross is God's way of saving men. There are those who say that they approach God in terms of philosophy—always stressing their search for God. To them the cross is not really essential. There are others who stress experience to the exclusion of everything else. Let me say that whatever their experience may be, if it is not based on the teaching of this book, they will find that they are being deluded by the evil one, who is ever ready to counterfeit a true experience.

The teaching concerning the cross is to be found everywhere in the Bible. Obviously the Book of Acts is the book to start with, for there, in a sense, we have an account of the first Christian preaching and teaching. In the sermon preached by Peter at Jerusalem after Pentecost, he made the point that our Lord's death was the result of "the determinate counsel and foreknowledge of God." In other words, he told the Jews that in one way they were not actually responsible for the death of Christ, though, in handing him over to the Roman authorities, they were the human instruments. Peter hinted that it was something that went right back into eternity; God is in this matter, he said. When you study the teaching of Paul in Acts you find that he does exactly the same thing. The key verses to the whole understanding of Paul's method are in chapter 17, where we are told that when he came to the synagogue at Thessalonica, he went in and ". . . reasoned with them out of the scriptures, Opening and alleging, that Christ must needs have suffered, and risen again from the dead; and that this Jesus, whom I preach unto you, is Christ" (vv. 2–3). Paul was addressing people who knew the Old Testament scriptures, but whose ideas concerning the Messiah were so confused that he says the cross was a stumbling block to them; they had never realized that Christ "must needs have suffered." Paul sought to prove to them that the Messiah whom they were expecting according to the Old Testament prophecies, was the Savior who had died.

The cross is the central teaching of all the Epistles. An attempt has been made to separate Paul's Epistles from the rest, and to suggest that this emphasis on the cross is peculiar to his teaching. But the fact is that all the apostles preach the same thing. Peter reminds those to whom he is writing that they have been redeemed, not with silver or gold, but by the blood of Christ. And John in an Epistle writes, "If we confess our sins he is faithful and just to forgive us our sins, and to cleanse us from all unrighteous-

ness." The teaching concerning the cross is also to be found
in the Book of Revelation.

The Cross in the Gospels

Someone will ask, "But what about the Gospels?" In
recent years the idea has been put forward that in the
Gospels there is little, if any, of this teaching at all; instead,
the claim is made that Paul, with his legalistic mind,
converted the simple teaching of Christ into a kind of
mythology, foisting certain Jewish legalistic notions on that
simple teaching.

The answer to this charge is twofold. One does not *expect*
to find as much teaching about the cross in the Gospels as is
found in Acts and the Epistles. Remember how our Lord one
day said to his disciples, "I have many things to say unto
you, but ye cannot bear them now"; if that applies to one
thing more than anything else, it is surely to the fact of his
death. When Christ did mention his death to the disciples
they were shocked and invariably failed to understand it. In
fact, the records show that it was not until after the
resurrection that they began to see the meaning of the cross
at all. When our Lord joined the two men on the road to
Emmaus, he showed them from the Scriptures how "Christ
must needs have suffered" that man's redemption might be
achieved.

Though we do not expect to find very much direct
teaching concerning the cross in the Gospels, actually there
is a great deal of teaching to be found there. John the Baptist
said, "Behold, the Lamb of God which taketh away the sins
of the world." And there is no more directly theological
statement concerning the meaning of the cross than that
found in the tenth chapter of Mark: "For even the Son of
man came not to be ministered unto, but to minister, and to
give his life a ransom for many" (v. 45).

Not only is this teaching found in the whole of the New
Testament, it is found in the Old Testament also, both in its

direct prophecies and in its types and adumbrations. Why was the offering of Abel more acceptable to God than that of Cain? There is only one answer: it was a blood offering. What is the real meaning of the story of Abraham and Isaac? Can it be adequately explained except as a foreshadowing of the one who was himself to be sacrificed on the cross— God's only begotten Son? The detailed instruction in regard to the tabernacle, with all its ritual and ceremony, is meaningless except as it speaks to us of the cross. How can you explain the various feasts, especially the Passover, apart from Calvary? Therefore I believe that the cross is God's method of saving men because it is clearly taught in the Bible.

The moment one accepts the teaching about the cross one finds innumerable reasons within oneself that support the teaching. Why do I believe that the cross is God's way of saving men in terms of reason and understanding, in addition to accepting the revelation? Why did God allow his Son to die on the cross? Because there was no other way. With our modern loose ideas of love we think that to forgive is a very simple matter, and yet to forgive, according to Paul, is a mighty problem, even to God. Why? Because of God's holy nature. God is holy and righteous. How can he at one and the same time be just, and the justifier of the ungodly? How can God forgive the sinner, and, at the same time, punish sin which leads to death? There is only one way, the way of the cross. Christ received our punishment, and in him we receive the forgiveness of God. It is what God did on Calvary that redeems me from sin. The cross is an eternal transaction between the Father and the Son. So my reasoning concerning this matter confirms revelation.

The Witness of Sin

If the cross is essential from God's aspect, it is equally essential from man's aspect. It is only at the cross that I realize what sin means—and I can never be saved unless I do realize what sin means. Sin is not just missing the mark; it is much more terrible than that. Sin is such a terrible thing that the Son of God had to die to redeem men from its power. I am helpless to deliver myself from it. What is the good of my trying to save myself by my good works? If man could have saved himself by his own efforts, then Christ need never have come. But he has come, and he has died. In the cross I see not only my helplessness, but I see also my salvation, and I know that in him I am accepted.

The same is true with regard to the power of sin. How can I be set free from its power? The answer is still to be found in the cross. There I see one who is powerful enough to keep me from falling. He has conquered sin, and death, and he can hold me fast in the hour of temptation. Indeed, it is only as I look at the cross that I learn to hate sin, for I am told concerning the cross that I have been bought with a price, the price of his own lifeblood, and that I am no longer my own.

The cross, therefore, is God's way of saving men. Only the cross can satisfy the demands of God and the needs of men. I join the great Apostle, and with humility say, "God forbid that I should glory save in the cross of our Lord Jesus Christ."

11

Sin and Its Consequences

And the mixt multitude that was among them fell a lusting: and the children of Israel also wept again, and said, Who shall give us flesh to eat? We remember the fish, which we did eat in Egypt freely; the cucumbers, and the melons, and the leeks, and the onions, and the garlick. But now our soul is dried away: there is nothing at all, beside this manna, before our eyes. (Num. 11:4–6)

I want to call attention to a particular incident in the history of the children of Israel that through it we may consider together the question of sin. Were I to deal with sin in a purely theological or academic manner there might be some people who would say, "Well, of course, that is probably all right for those who are interested in that kind of subject, but it has little to do with us." Such a response is precluded by the discussion of the sin question in terms of an actual event occurring in the lives of actual people. Given such circumstances, it becomes impossible for us to consider this a purely theoretical matter, one in which we may or may not choose to be interested in.

Preached in Westminster Chapel

87

As we approach this subject of sin, I can imagine someone else saying, ''Surely you are not going to spend your time in discussing a purely negative subject like this? Why not deal with something positive? Surely you are not going to be ensnared by something characteristic of the Puritans? Instead of spending your time describing and dissecting something that is ugly and black and foul, it would be much better if you spent your time in telling us about the goodness of Jesus or the love of God, in calling us to consider beauty and truth.''

Such an attitude denotes an entirely false view of preaching. Implicit in such criticism is the suggestion that preaching should always give men what they desire rather than what they need. There is the feeling that men have a right to demand certain things of the messengers of God. That is a popular view of preaching, and I have no doubt that it accounts largely for the state of the world today. We have all probably at some time or another found ourselves in a dentist's chair, and we have resented the pain that he caused us; we may even have grabbed his hand in an attempt to restrain him. But he knows that his task is to do not that which is pleasing to us but that which is ultimately for our good. Temporary suffering is often essential to permanent healing.

Precisely the same thing is true in regard to the preaching of the gospel. No preacher of the Word of God really rejoices in saying things that are unpleasant; but if he is true to his commission, and if his concern is to proclaim the whole counsel of God, there are times when he must do so.

In addition, it is always a very foolish argument to imagine that you can immediately proceed to the positive thing without first dealing with that which is negative. What would you think of a man suffering from some complaint who said to his physician, ''Now, doctor, I do not want you to examine me. What I want you to do is to give me something to ease my pain''? I think you would agree that such a man could only be described by one word—used in a proper sense. You would say that he was a fool. Precisely the same thing is true of anyone who objects to a discussion of the great question of sin. The patient's trouble was that he thought all that was necessary was the relief of his pain. Those who object to the preaching of sin will tell you that their whole view concerning that subject is light and superficial. They of all people are the ones who most need such a message.

Man holds a fundamentally wrong view of sin, and this shows itself in two main directions. He tends to regard sin merely as something touching his actions and his activities. He looks upon it as a mere headache, instead of as a foul disease. A headache may be nothing but a passing ailment with no real significance at all; on the other hand, it may be a sign of something profoundly wrong with a man's whole system. The tendency is to regard sin as something on the circumference of life, when all the time it is a rank disease attacking the very vitals of human nature: as though sin was something attacking our very nature. This is why, in ordinary parlance, we frequently hear the expression concerning a man that though he may be living an evil life, yet he has a good heart. It is for this reason that there have been so many violent objections raised to preaching that concerns sin and the need for rebirth and conversion. This, therefore, is the question which must be faced: Which of these two views of sin is the right one—the modern view of it, or the biblical view that declares sin an evil principle that tarnishes and spoils life at its very source?

Obviously it is impossible in one sermon to deal exhaustively with the subject; but as we study this incident in the story of the children of Israel we shall learn certain things that are always true of sin. Let us examine ourselves as we look into their story, for the deliverance of the children of Israel from Egyptian bondage is a portrayal of the salvation which Christ accomplished for mankind. While this Old Testament story has historical significance, at the same time it is a perfect picture of what God offers to do in Christ for those who are willing to trust him.

We see in the Numbers incident the nature of sin from three different standpoints. First, the story reveals the utter folly of sin, describing it as a form of madness. The Bible teaches that sin is something which affects the mind of man; sin's tragedy is that it affects man in his highest faculties. There are numerous statements to that effect both in the Old and New Testaments. Isaiah puts it, ''The ox knoweth his owner, and the ass his master's crib: but Israel doth not know, my people doth not consider'' (1:3). Jeremiah says something very similar: ''Yea, the stork in the heaven knoweth her appointed times; and the turtle and the crane and the swallow observe the time of their coming; but my people know not the judgment of the LORD'' (8:7). The animals seem to understand; man alone seems to be foolish. The animals act by instinct; but God has made man greater than the animals. He has given man reasoning powers; yet it is there that man fails thereby bringing himself not only to the level of the animals, but also lower than the animals. That is the folly of sin.

In our passage the children of Israel express a longing to be back again in Egypt. Is it possible that these people, after enduring the lashes of their taskmasters, and watching their children massacred, could look back on that life with anything but abhorrence? Yet that is exactly what they did. There is only one way to describe such an attitude: unutterable folly. And that is the characteristic of sin. A man does something that is wrong and he suffers as a result. You would think that he would never again return to such a way of living, yet he does the same thing again, the very thing that has caused him pain and remorse. Sin causes us to become fools; it makes us behave in an unreasonable, irrational manner.

When we study the question further, we see the element of disillusion that is always present with sin. That is the only explanation for the fact that the children of Israel could conceivably look back with longing to those days spent in

Egypt. Sin had so affected them that they remembered nothing but the fish, the cucumbers, the melons, the leeks, and the onions they once enjoyed there. There is no mention of their taskmasters, nor of the massacre of their children. Sin deludes a man by reminding him only of that which is pleasant, and by obliterating from his memory the distasteful things. To consider only the pleasant elements in a situation and deliberately ignore the unpleasant things is surely a sign of an intellect that is functioning in a very low and unworthy manner.

Sin is folly, but the height of the folly is that a man in such a position, far from thanking anyone who tries to show him his folly, generally resents the advice and refuses to listen to reason. Are we living our lives on a rational basis? Do we think about our actions in a logical manner? Are we interested only in those things which we like and enjoy—the cucumbers, the melons, the leeks, and the onions? The second characteristic of sin is its perverting effect. Sin twists our very nature. It is not merely something that affects the mind and the understanding; it affects the very center of our being. It is not only that man does not *do* what God asks; it is that he *rejects* what God wants him to do. Or as Jesus put it, out of the heart comes evil thoughts.

This perverting effect of sin is very evident in the story of the children of Israel. It was not only that they desired the good things of Egypt; the seriousness of their sin is to be seen in their attitude toward the manna. They said, "But now our soul is dried away; there is nothing at all, beside this manna, before our eyes." There is scorn and derision in their words. They despised the manna sent from heaven. Consider the ignorance displayed in such an attitude. The sending of manna from heaven is one of the most remarkable miracles of the Old Testament, yet these people seemed to think that the cucumbers and onions of Egypt were infinitely superior to this miraculous bread from God. Thus we see the perverting effect of sin in its very essence. Why did the Greeks regard the gospel as folly? Because they preferred to use their own understanding rather than accept the free gift of God. Why was the cross a stumbling block to the Jews? Because they preferred to try to please God, by their own good works, and refused to accept the gift of salvation through the sacrifice of Christ. What would you think of a man who insisted on attempting the impossible rather than accepting that which has been accomplished for him? Surely, you would say that such a man was, by nature, perverted. Yet that is the position of all who reject the gospel of our Lord and Savior Jesus Christ. Men prefer to work out their own salvation rather than accept God's free gift.

The Israelites' statement regarding the manna reveals not only ignorance, but also arrogance. They contemptuously referred to "this manna!" In other words, they despised this miraculous gift of God—and that, alas, is another characteristic of sin. As you read about the crucifixion, you see how the sarcasm, the scorn, the derision of the people was poured out on Jesus as he hung on the cross. It was there they manifested their hatred of him. At the cross they revealed their real nature. There is nothing that calls forth so much ridicule and scorn than what men call "this salvation business," this preaching of the cross. It is there that the perversion of sin is seen at its worst. It is the supernatural element in the gospel that has always constituted the greatest stumbling block to the natural man. The children of Israel had been brought out of Egypt into safety, and God had provided manna for them to eat, yet all the time they desired the melons and onions of Egypt. These people felt that life in Egypt was much better than wandering in the wilderness. People today say, "Belief in God is all right, but the Christian life is so narrow." That is the objection. No man wants to go to hell. The objection is not in regard to the ultimate safety. It is the Christian life that has to be lived in the meantime. Men still prefer the temporal—the pleasures of a dying world—to the ways of Jesus.

The most terrible thing about sin is its base ingratitude. Look at the attitude of the children of Israel toward God who had delivered them from the bondage of Egypt. He had raised up Moses to lead them. He had brought them safely through the Red Sea. But time and again they rebelled against him. And here we find them referring contemptuously to "this manna," as if God's gift to them was something unworthy. Oh, the base ingratitude of it all! Could anything be worse?

But there is something even worse. For God has sent into the world, not manna, but the very Son of his love. Jesus came from heaven and voluntarily bore our sins in his own body on the tree. He died our death; he was buried in our place; and he rose again for our justification. Yet masses of men and women not only reject him but refuse him, and they do so with scorn and sarcasm and derision. Oh, the terrible ingratitude of it all!

Let us look at ourselves in the light of this Old Testament incident, and if there is any element of that same attitude still lingering in us, may we repent of it once and for all, with shame and contrition, and may we turn to God and seek his forgiveness through Jesus Christ our Lord.

12

The Meaning of the Resurrection

*That if thou shalt confess with thy mouth the Lord
Jesus, and shalt believe in thine heart that God hath
raised him from the dead, thou shalt be saved.*
(Rom. 10:9)

There is a sense in which it is important, on
these special occasions in the calendar of the church, not so
much to preach as to call attention to great facts, and
perhaps to underline their significance. Human nature, as a
result of sin, is prone to forget the real centralities of the
faith. The history of the church demonstrates very clearly,
alas, that there is nothing which is quite so easy, or so simple,
as to drift away from the stand which we once made in
Christ to something lower, something incomplete. Indeed,
there is a very real danger of our proceeding along that path,
perhaps quite unconsciously, to such an extent that we end
by believing that which is not actually faith at all.

And so, there is nothing more important than pausing
from time to time to examine ourselves as to whether or not

Preached in Westminster Chapel

95

we be in the faith—to use the words of Paul in writing to the church at Corinth. These special days in the church calendar force us to do that—that is, if we regard them aright. But if we spend our time saying that the resurrection helps us to believe that when things are black they may suddenly become bright, or that the whole of nature teaches us that death leads to life—then while we may encourage one another in so doing, and make ourselves buoyant in spirit, we shall not really be examining ourselves, and it will have nothing to do with the Christian faith. That is one of the dangers which always confronts us—the danger of turning this wondrous faith into a mere collection of optimistic ideas, a mere source of good cheer—that might be equally well provided by a host of other things.

More than a Philosophy

We cannot face a time like the present without realizing certain things about our faith, without realizing its tremendous importance and value. One thing of which we are reminded is that Christianity is not a philosophy, an idea concerning life; it is a religion, and is based solidly on historical facts. That is fundamental.

There are many religions in the world which are, in the last analysis, nothing but philosophies, points of view with respect to life. If you read the account of the first preaching of the disciples you will find that they did not go about seeking to establish a new order. They went about stating facts; they regarded themselves as messengers. Paul, in a picturesque phrase, refers to himself as a kind of billposter, announcing certain facts to the people. You can put facts on a hoarding (billboard). You can make an announcement on a hoarding. You cannot put a philosophy on a hoarding. That is the first thing to bear in mind about the Christian faith. It is not, primarily, a philosophy. It is based on definite, historic facts.

A Matter of Salvation

Writing to the Romans, Paul reminds the reader that a person's attitude toward those historic facts is a matter on which his salvation rests: "If thou shalt confess with thy mouth the Lord Jesus, and shalt believe in thine heart that God hath raised him from the dead, thou shalt be saved." The resurrection is not a fact that we can afford to study in a careless or cursory manner, for it is a fact that ultimately judges us. According to the teaching of the New Testament, to believe or not to believe in these facts determines the whole of a man's eternal future. When we face the fact of the resurrection in this serious way, we are driven to self-examination; we are forced to look at where we stand. We ask ourselves, What place has it in my life and experience? What part is it playing in my daily life? Does it really occupy the center of my being? Is my life governed by it? Special days force us to face such questions. And, according to Paul, of all the historical facts contained in the New Testament, the most important of all is the fact of the resurrection. What is the gospel in its essence? It is to believe in one's heart the fact of the resurrection. Paul's acid test for any individual professing Christianity is, What does he or she believe about the resurrection? I wonder how many of us would have made that choice had we been asked to make such an acid test. Some of us would have said, What does he think of the life of Christ, of his teaching, of his miracles? But Paul says, Here is the central thing—to believe in one's heart that God has raised Jesus from the dead. And a person can only confess with his mouth that which he has first of all believed.

Why does the apostle make our belief in the resurrection the acid test of our faith? In general, because none of the other things is sufficient. Christ's life and death, his teaching and his miracles, all have their importance but not one of them is sufficient in and of itself. Do we believe that God has raised Jesus from the dead? That is the acid test. If you read the Book of Acts you will find that the one fact in the forefront of the disciples' preaching was the fact of the resurrection. You will find it in the sermon preached by Peter on Pentecost, and it is emphasized in the message of Paul given in Pisidia (13:30–34).

Why did they make the fact of the resurrection the ultimate test? Because it is this fact, and this fact alone, that really proves who Jesus is. It is the resurrection that declares that he is indeed the very Son of God.

Surely we are entitled to say that it was the fact of the resurrection that ultimately convinced the disciples. Peter made his great confession of faith at Caesarea Philippi, but we know he subsequently fell from it. And we remember that all the disciples, at the time of the crucifixion, forsook Jesus and fled. It was only when they saw him risen from the dead that they realized he was truly the Son of God. It was true not only of Thomas, but also of all the disciples, that when the women reported to them that Jesus had risen, it seemed to them but idle tales.

As for Paul, he had been an unbeliever and had perse-cuted the church. Then on the road to Damascus he met the risen Lord and became a witness to the resurrection. He had no claim to be an apostle unless he could bear witness to the resurrection. This is the most vital thing of all, for unless we are right as to who Christ is, we can understand nothing at all about him. If you find difficulty in believing in the miracles of Jesus, get right first about his person. Once you realize that he is the Son of God you will expect the unusual to happen. There is a sense in which you cannot understand his works except in the light of his person. And there is nothing that so definitely attests to who he is as the fact of the resurrection.

Prophecy Fulfilled

In the Old Testament there were certain predictions made that Christ would rise from the grave. In Psalms 16 and 110 there are prophecies concerning the resurrection. The same occurs in Isaiah 53. There are these foreshadowings that the Messiah, when he came, would be crucified, that he would die and be buried, and that he would rise from the dead. It is only of Jesus Christ that we can say that his body did not see corruption.

The resurrection also substantiates what our Lord predicted concerning himself. He told his disciples that he would suffer at the hands of cruel men, but he always added that he would rise again the third day. The fact that the disciples did not accept it makes no difference to the argument. Jesus himself predicted it, and his actual rising from the dead proves it.

Also of importance is the fact that the resurrection of Christ from the dead is altogether different than the rising from the dead of Lazarus, of the daughter of Jairus, and of the son of the widow of Nain. The latter were, in a sense, merely revivified. They came back to life but subsequently they died again. Theirs was but a temporary return to life, a reanimation. There has been no one else of whom it can be said that he came forth from death to die no more, save the Son of God. There is also another fact of great importance in this connection; after the resurrection Christ's body was clearly glorified. He possessed the same body. It bore the imprint of the nails and the wound in his side caused by the spear; yet it was different. Jesus came in despite the closed door, and at first the disciples did not recognize him. His body had already taken on the process of glorification. From all this I go on to draw a deduction. It is the resurrection that shows the true meaning of Jesus' death, and that is a most important point. I do not hesitate to affirm, on the basis of the New Testament teaching, that no one can possibly understand the meaning of the death of Christ who does not believe in the fact of the resurrection. He who died is the Son of God. His death was not something brought about by man. He could have avoided it had he chosen so to do. He could, had he wished, have defeated the evil designs of the scribes and Pharisees. And yet he was crucified. Why? When I realize that the one who died on the cross was the Son of God, I have my eyes opened to the New Testament doctrine of the atonement, which tells me that

> There was no other good enough
> To pay the price of sin.
> He only could unlock the gate
> Of heaven, and let me in.

He alone was the perfect, spotless offering. In the words of Paul to the Corinthians, "[God] hath made him to be sin for us, who knew no sin; that we might be made the righteousness of God in him" (2 Cor. 5:21).

The Only Way to Certainty

Furthermore, it is only in the light of the resurrection that I see the sufficiency of his death. We may be tempted to ask: Can one die for all? Has the power of death been vanquished? It is only in the fact of the resurrection that I know for certain. That is why I must believe in the resurrection. If I did not, I should still be in doubt about the forgiveness of my sins. But if I believe that God has, indeed, raised Christ from the dead, then I can say in the language of Paul, "Who is he that condemneth? It is Christ that died, yea, rather, that is risen again." It is the fact of the resurrection that ultimately convinces and convicts me of sin. If you would realize the necessity of salvation, then you must go to the resurrection. It is only on the cross that sin is dealt with, it is only thus that we are reconciled to God.

So we find abundant reasons for putting the resurrection into the first position. We see why it must be made the acid test. There is nothing so clearly established as the fact of the resurrection. Someone has said that it is the best-attested fact of history, and there can be no doubt about it. The proofs of the resurrection are indisputable. But the danger is that we be content with a mere historical view of it. No, says Paul, we must believe it in the heart: theologically, not merely historically. And to believe it in the heart means that it becomes the governing factor in our lives, and because of that we count it our highest privilege to confess it with our lips before men.

13

Sounding the Alarm

Watch ye. . . . (1 Cor. 16:13)

There is nothing so characteristic of Paul as the way in which he constantly breaks in on the matter at hand. Suddenly some inspiration seems to come to him, and he interpolates something which seems to be quite extraneous; but when we come to examine these interpolations we find that invariably they are perfectly logical. We find the selfsame thing as we look at our text. Paul lays a basis; then he builds on it; then he adds to it. His tactics are very definitely worked out in a given plan. And here you have the first step.

"Watch ye," says the apostle. If you prefer another translation quite a number could be suggested. The phrase "Watch ye" might also read "Wake up!" or "Be wakeful!" Or adopting military terminology, it would not be inappropriate if we translated the phrase "Attention!" For this is exactly what the apostle is seeking. He wants to rouse his readers, to awaken them, to keep them in a condition of watchfulness.

Preached in a Westminster Chapel

Another way of translating Paul's exhortation would be to borrow from the language of the Old Testament "Sound the alarm!" Or, we might say that in using these words, the apostle is really ordering someone to sound the reveille, announcing to the troops that they must wake up, put on their uniforms, and go each man to his post to stand and watch.

"Watch Ye!"

The expression, *Watch ye,* is thoroughly typical not only of the New Testament but also of the Old. If you read the various discourses of Jesus you will find that he often utters the word *watch.* Not only is this exhortation characteristic of the last chapters of the Gospels, it is found very frequently in the Epistles as well. It also seems to be the theme above every other theme in the Book of Revelation.

This exhortation to watch, to stand at attention, to mount guard is one that Christian people stand constantly in need of hearing. Such an exhortation is never frequently repeated in Scripture without it being perfectly obvious that it is a word that was needed. Our Lord would never have repeated his exhortation to watch if he had not realized the dangers that were going to confront his people. And so he sought to prepare them.

Never in the history of the Christian church has this word been more needed than at this present hour. There have been times of lethargy in the past; there have been dark periods in history when the church has been more or less decadent. But there has never been a time when we stood in need of this word more than we do today.

Why Do We Watch?

Why does this mighty Christian general command us to watch, to be on guard? The immediate New Testament answer is that there is need of watchfulness for the simple reason that the Christian life is a life of conflict. That is an idea with which we've become, to a large extent, unfamiliar. How often do we conceive of the Christian life as a battle, a warfare? Or of the church as a fighting force left here on earth by God himself? I suggest that the Christian church has lost sight of this vital New Testament truth. If we are to correct that impression, it behooves us to discover the reasons why such a truth has been lost, for we cannot put ourselves right without discovering why we went wrong.

What are the reasons?

Surely one of the explanations is that there has been a tendency for many years now to exclude the supernatural from religion. And in exactly the same way there has been a tendency not to believe in the power of Satan and those unseen evil forces at work in the world today. Once we lose sight of the spiritual nature of life, we must of necessity lose this idea of a spiritual conflict.

To put it another way, there has been a tendency to regard Christianity as being nothing but a philosophy, an outlook on life. Instead of thinking of it as something that covers all aspects and departments of life, man sees it simply as a philosophy which he can either accept or reject. And as you do not expect to find a dynamic force in a philosophy, so men have argued that there is no such thing in Christianity.

Again, many people have thought of Christianity solely in terms of a life to be lived, as something purely practical. I think of the emphasis on the social application of the gospel in recent years: if we think of the gospel merely in these practical terms, we shall of necessity lose the idea of a mighty spiritual conflict between good and evil, between God and Satan, between heaven and hell—which is the characteristic teaching of the New Testament.

Others, I fear, have lost the sense of the Christian life as a conflict because they tend to regard it as a passive state of relaxation.

A Life of Struggle

If the New Testament does one thing more than another, it surely emphasizes that the Christian life is a battle. Toward the end of his life, Paul speaks about the good fight of faith; he tells us that the Christian life is a life of wrestling. Peter says that our adversary is like a roaring lion seeking whom he may devour. The preeminent message in the Book of Revelation is the message of spiritual powers battling, as it were, for this world and for mankind.

This impression of the Christian life is abundantly confirmed by all the great Christian literature of the ages. If you examine it, especially that written during times of revival, you will find that it always emphasizes this idea of a spiritual conflict. (In John Bunyan's *Pilgrim's Progress*, for example, we see a pilgrim beset by enemies: it is a fight for the city of Mansoul.) We are to fight because the Christian life is essentially a conflict. And we are to fight for this further reason, that, according to the New Testament, if we do not fight, we shall be vanquished; we shall fall victim to the enemy.

What Do We Watch?

What are we to watch? The answer is simple. First, I am to watch myself. Anyone who has not yet discovered that he himself is his greatest problem, especially in the Christian life, is just a novice in these matters. Before you watch anyone else, watch yourself.

"What am I to watch in myself?" you ask. First of all, watch against a lowered general morale: Am I beginning to feel a little bit hopeless about the church and its message? I see the masses of the people going everywhere but to God's house. I see a lowering of the moral tone. Do I ask myself whether it is worthwhile going on with it? Am I as spiritually keen and alert as I once was?

I have to watch myself against the constant danger of a lowered standard in connection with my own life. There was a time when I believed in making a clean cut. There were certain things which I said were not legitimate to me because I was a Christian. I recognized certain standards in the matter of honesty and chastity. I had a certain standard of morality. Am I as sensitive to sin as I once was? Or is there on my part a tendency to compromise in regard to my sins? Have I become an expert in explaining away what I do? Have I become an expert in the work of self-justification? We must watch constantly against a lowering of the standard.

In exactly the same way we must ever be watching ourselves lest there be a lowering of our strength, and of our efficiency. Am I taking my spiritual exercise regularly? Do I find when I meet temptation that I can resist it with the same ease that I used to? Have I the same reserves of power on which to call in the hour of subtle temptation? Has there come a lowering of strength because of the lessened exercise of my spiritual faculties? I know there is nothing easier than to let the days pass, forgetting these things. Life is so full and active; we say we haven't time to read God's Word, or to meditate on spiritual things. We are so ready to make excuses for our neglect.

Having watched myself, I must also watch the enemy: It would be useless for a man to watch himself without also keeping an eye on the enemy. And the first thing we must watch is his strength and power. Some people seem to think that the whole of spiritual conflict centers around things residing in the flesh, but let us never forget that our conflict is against mighty *spiritual* forces.

Over and above the power of the enemy is the subtlety of the enemy. Paul reminds us that Satan can transform himself into a veritable angel of light in his effort to pull us from the truth which is in Christ Jesus our Lord. This is a vitally important matter today. The greatest danger that confronts the present-day church is the danger of allowing herself to be sidetracked, of putting all the emphasis on secondary matters. Let us read the Word of God, let us interpret prophecy, let us understand sanctification, let us be concerned about Christian education—let us do all these things, but let us always remember that the primary business and function of the church is to call men to repentance, to denounce the sin and evil which is at the root of all our problems, to preach Christ and him crucified, and to make contact with fallen humanity.

When Do We Watch?

Finally, when am I to watch? I am to watch always. There is nothing so dangerous as to leave the watching until something has happened. I must watch now. I must watch always. There is no such thing as a spiritual holiday. I must always be on duty. I must ever be on the alert. "I must be instant in season and out of season."

14

Living Near to God

For, lo, they that are far from thee shall perish. . . .
But it is good for me to draw near to God: I have
put my trust in the Lord GOD, that I may declare all
thy works. (Ps. 73:27–28)

These final two verses of Psalm 73 are not only
the actual conclusion to the Psalm and its message, but are
also the conclusion at which their author has arrived as a
result of the experiences he has just described. Verses 27
and 28 are his final meditation; he has finished his review of
the past, and as he faces the future he resolves that, as far as
he is concerned, there is one thing that he is going to do:
draw near to God.

This is one of the great values of the Psalms; their authors
not only passed through certain experiences in life, but also
recorded them, along with their reactions to them, and
then, as a result of all that happened, laid down certain
principles.

The experience of the psalmist is one with which we are
familiar: he had been most unhappy. As he looked around it

Preached in Westminster Chapel

seemed to him that the ungodly people flourished—and that set him thinking. He began wondering whether, after all, there was any purpose in being godly. He was tempted to ask, Is God just? Is there any point in trying to walk the narrow way? He was in real trouble until he went to the house of God; then God opened his eyes and gave him a correct perspective of life. God revealed to him the fact that he was still ready to bless him. And this man then saw how arrogant he had been, and he began to praise and worship God. It was in this way that he arrived at his conclusion. I wonder whether, as we face the unknown future, we have come to the same conclusion, and made the same resolve: "It is good for me to draw near to God." The psalmist's words could also be translated, "Nearness to God is good for me." In the future this particular man's ambition is going to be just that—to keep near to God.

Where Everything Goes Wrong—or Right

The psalmist helps us to see the importance of his resolve by putting it in the form of a contrast: "For, lo, they that are far from thee shall perish," but "Nearness to God is good for me." We are either far from God or we are near to him; there is no other position possible. This man concluded, "What has really been wrong with me is that I have not kept near to God. I've been given this enlightenment in the sanctuary of God." He realized that there was only one thing that mattered—a man's relationship with God.

We all tend to think that our happiness depends on certain things in life. The sight of the ungodly and their apparent prosperity had made this man envious, and he began to grumble and complain. He now sees that his unhappiness was due to one thing only—the fact that he hadn't kept near to God. This is the beginning and the end of wisdom in the Christian life. The moment we get away from God everything will go wrong. It is exactly like a ship crossing the Atlantic. If sight of the northern star is lost, the compass begins to go wrong. It is not the things the world regards as important that matter; for the Christian the important thing is to keep near to God. There we find joy and peace; there we rest confidently and securely in the arms of his love. Therefore, this is my resolve: I am going to live near to God; whatever else may happen in life, this to me will be the essential thing. How we should thank God more and more for his Word! The Bible never just gives us a great injunction; it always gives us the reason for such an injunction.

One reason for keeping near to God is to consider the fate of those who are living far from him. The psalmist realizes that it was the sight of the ungodly people around him that really led him astray, and he resolves not to fall into that trap again. "They that are far from thee shall perish." (Consider the story of Sodom and Gomorrah and the cities of the plain. How easily might Abraham have wondered whether it really paid to be godly!) But this psalmist comes to the conclusion that it doesn't matter what the temporary prosperity of the ungodly may be, for "they that are far from thee shall perish."

The Great Message of the Bible

That is the great message of this Book from beginning to end. We are called to view life as the heroes of the faith in the eleventh chapter of the Epistle to the Hebrews viewed it. We need to "esteem the reproach of Christ greater riches than all the treasures in Egypt." We must see this world under condemnation. It is all going to perish. It is vanity, it is emptiness. Moth and rust are in the very warp and woof of the most glittering prizes that the world has to offer.

"They that are far from thee shall perish." There is a terrible fate awaiting those who are far from God. Are we all perfectly clear about that, I wonder? Is your worship of God grudging? As you face the future is there any hesitation in your mind whether you should go on in the Christian life?

You see others who never worship God, but nothing seems to go wrong with them. There was a farmer who decided that he would harvest his crops on Sunday. He had marvelous crops, and soon his barns were filled to overflowing. And he told his minister when he met him on one occasion that his preaching must be wrong. "Calamity has not descended on me," he said. "My crops have not been destroyed. You told me of the consequences that I should have to face if I did not reverence God's Day. But what about your preaching now?" The old minister looked at the farmer, and simply said, "God does not always make up his accounts in the fall." The psalmist says, "It is good for me to draw near to God." I resolve that I will live my life as near to God as I possibly can.

Why? Because of the character of God. If we fully realized that, there would be nothing we would desire more in this world than just to be in his presence. We like to be in the presence of people we love. We like to be introduced to people who are considered great in various ways. But how loath we are to spend our time in the presence of God! The psalmist here is emphasizing God's sovereignty, his greatness and majesty: the everlasting, the eternal God, the Creator of the heavens and the earth, the Lord Jehovah, the covenant-keeping God.

When he called Moses to lead the children of Israel out of captivity, God gave Moses a special revelation of himself as Jehovah. God is concerned about the welfare of his children; he pledges and binds himself to us. Now, says the psalmist, I want above everything else in life to keep near to such a God; I want to keep in touch with him.

We would be grateful if some great person were to say to us, "I am going to keep in touch with you." We would see it is a privilege and an honor. The Lord Jesus Christ came to reveal the Father to us. He said, ". . . that they might know thee the only true God, and Jesus Christ, whom thou hast sent" (John 17:3). As John puts it in his Epistle, "Our fellowship is with the Father." This is what the psalmist desired above everything else, to live always in the presence of God.

What an uplifting thought this is! We do not know what is awaiting us. We live in a world that is full of change, and we ourselves are changeable creatures. In this world there is instability, uncertainty. Is there anything more wonderful than to know that at any moment we can enter into the presence of one who is everlasting, "the Father of lights, with whom there is no variableness," whatever may be happening around us? He is always the same, in his might, in his majesty, in his glory, in his love, in his mercy. Let us realize that in Christ he offers us his fellowship, his companionship.

God Will Meet Us

"It is good for me to draw near to God." It is surprising that this man should say this in view of the experiences he had gone through. And it was not until he went into the sanctuary of God that his happiness came flooding back to him, and he was able to rejoice in God. "Draw nigh to God, and he will draw nigh to you," says James in his Epistle (4:8). Every time we take a step in the direction of God, he will take a step in our direction. If we approach God in faith we can be certain that he will approach us. He is the God of our salvation, and that is a good reason why we should draw near to him. He is the giver of every good and perfect gift. It is when I am near to God that I know my sins are forgiven. I am conscious of his love; I become possessed of a joy that the world can neither give, nor take away. Think of those moments of supreme peace and joy that you have experienced: have they not been moments when you have been near to God? In the presence of God you are lifted up above your circumstances. It is a place of blessing.

"It is good for me to draw near to God: I have put my trust in the Lord God." It is a place of safety. If there is one thing we all pray for as we look into the unknown future it is security. We feel that we have let ourselves down, and we ask ourselves, On whom can I repose my trust? Where can I find a sense of security? Only in God. "I have put my trust in the Lord God." The Psalms are full of this truth. "The name of the Lord is a strong tower." The evil one cannot touch us, for we are in Christ. Nothing can harm those who are in the safekeeping of their covenant-keeping God.

To Glorify Him

But the psalmist has still another reason for resolving to keep near to God: "that I may declare all thy works" and thereby I may glorify him. If I keep near to God, I shall experience his salvation; I shall possess this sense of security, and that will immediately lead me to praise and glorify his name before others. That is the point at which we must arrive. You remember the first question of the Shorter Catechism: "The chief end of man is to glorify God, and to enjoy him for ever." Yes, says this man, I am going to keep near to God that I may glorify him as well as enjoy his presence. And my business in life is to tell others about him by life and lip, in word and in action.

If we are to keep near to God we must live a life of communion with him. We must decide that we will no longer allow the world to take up our time and energy. It was when he went into the sanctuary of God that this man found peace and rest of soul. If you want to keep near to God, pray and read his Word not only in the privacy of your own room, but in fellowship with others. Take time for meditation, for thinking about God and spiritual things, and for practicing his presence. Do not give yourself any peace until you know that your sins are forgiven, until you are conscious as you pray that God is speaking to you. The other thing we must learn is to obey God. Those are the two rules to bear in mind—to seek God, and then to obey him. And if by reason of sin you feel that your communion with God has been broken, you immediately reestablish it by confessing your sin to him, knowing that "the blood of Jesus Christ cleanses us from all sin."

God grant that this may by our heartfelt resolve. "It is good for me to draw near to God." May we know him, and dwell with him, and spend the remainder of our days basking in the sunshine of his face, and enjoying his blessed companionship.